This Coloring Boo

ART

Between the Lines Volume 5

A Coloring Book by Contemporary Artists

Generously Sponsored by COACH

Cover Artwork by John Baldessari

RxArt is a nonprofit organization whose mission is to help children heal through the extraordinary power of visual art. We commission exceptional contemporary artists to transform sterile healthcare facilities into engaging and inspiring spaces full of beauty, humor and comfort.

Artists

Rita Ackermann

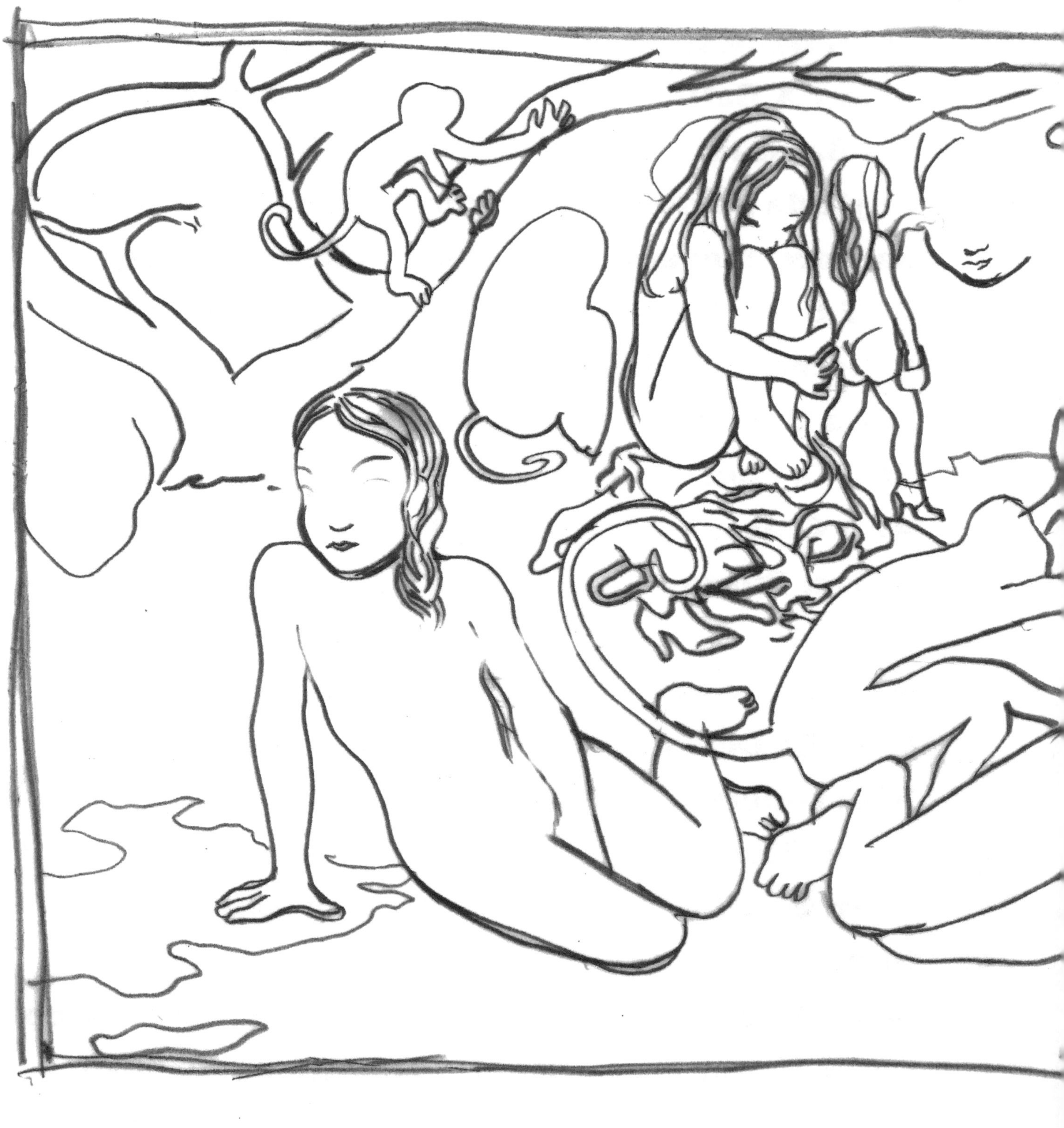

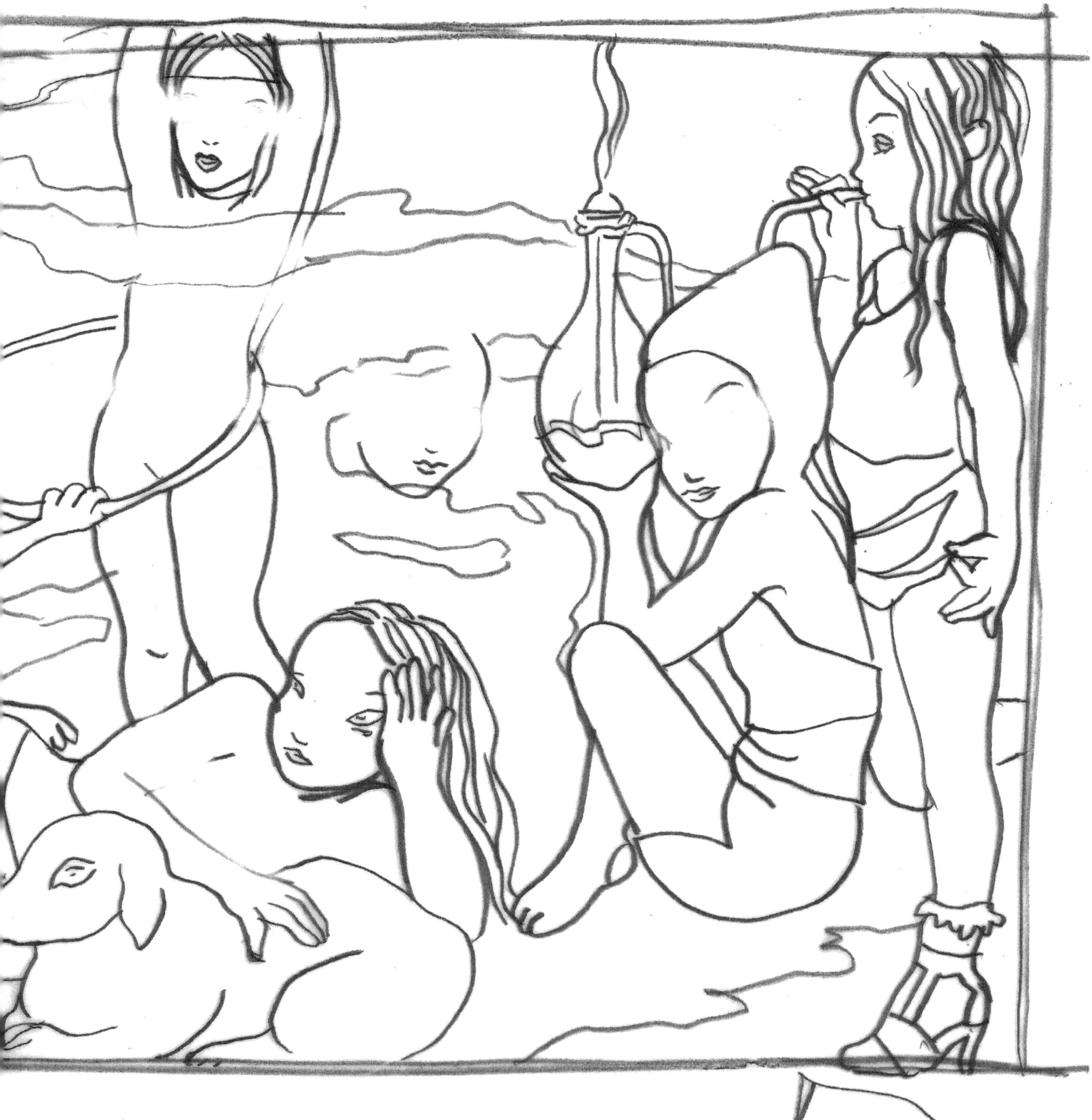

Afruz Amighi

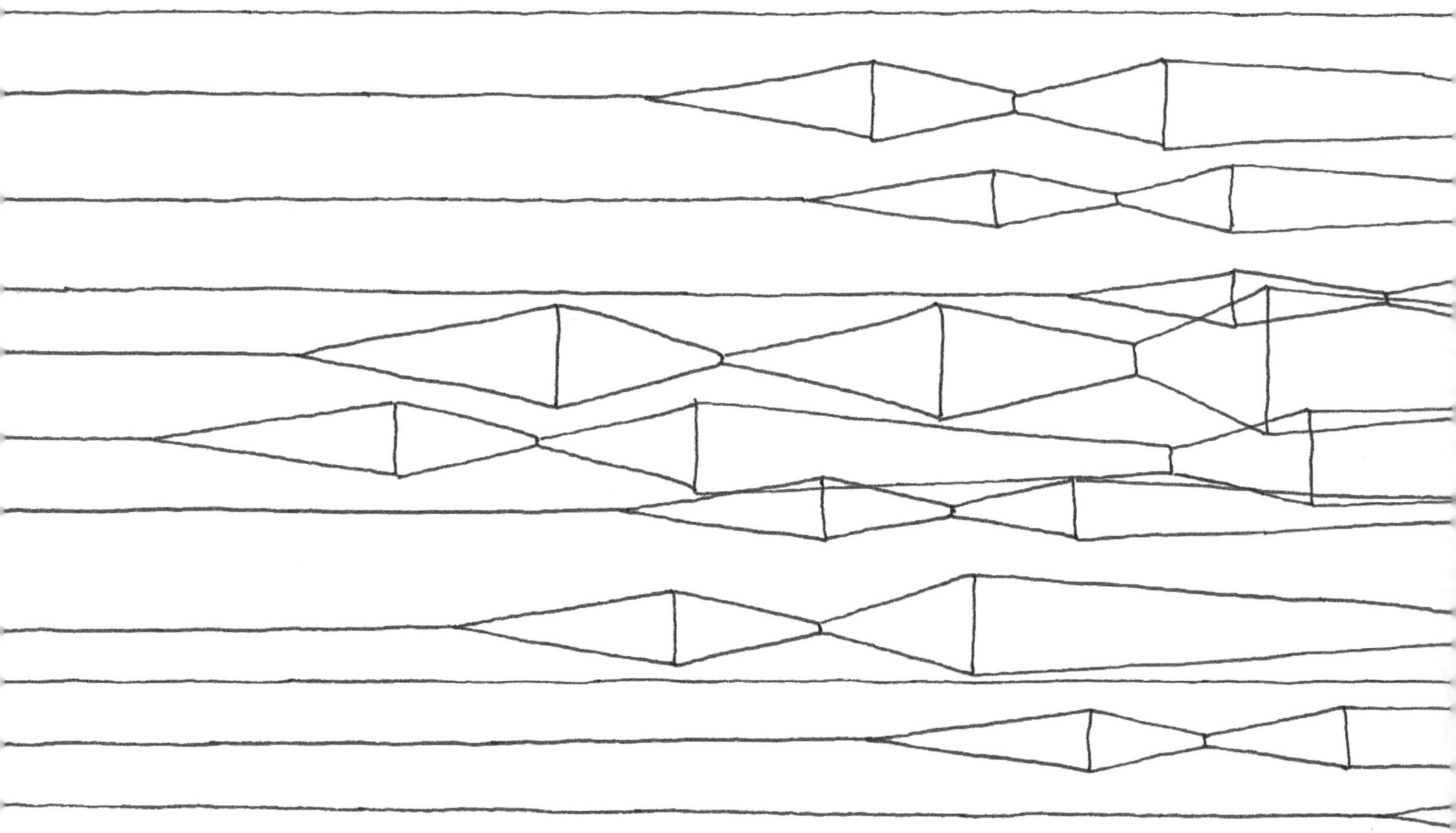

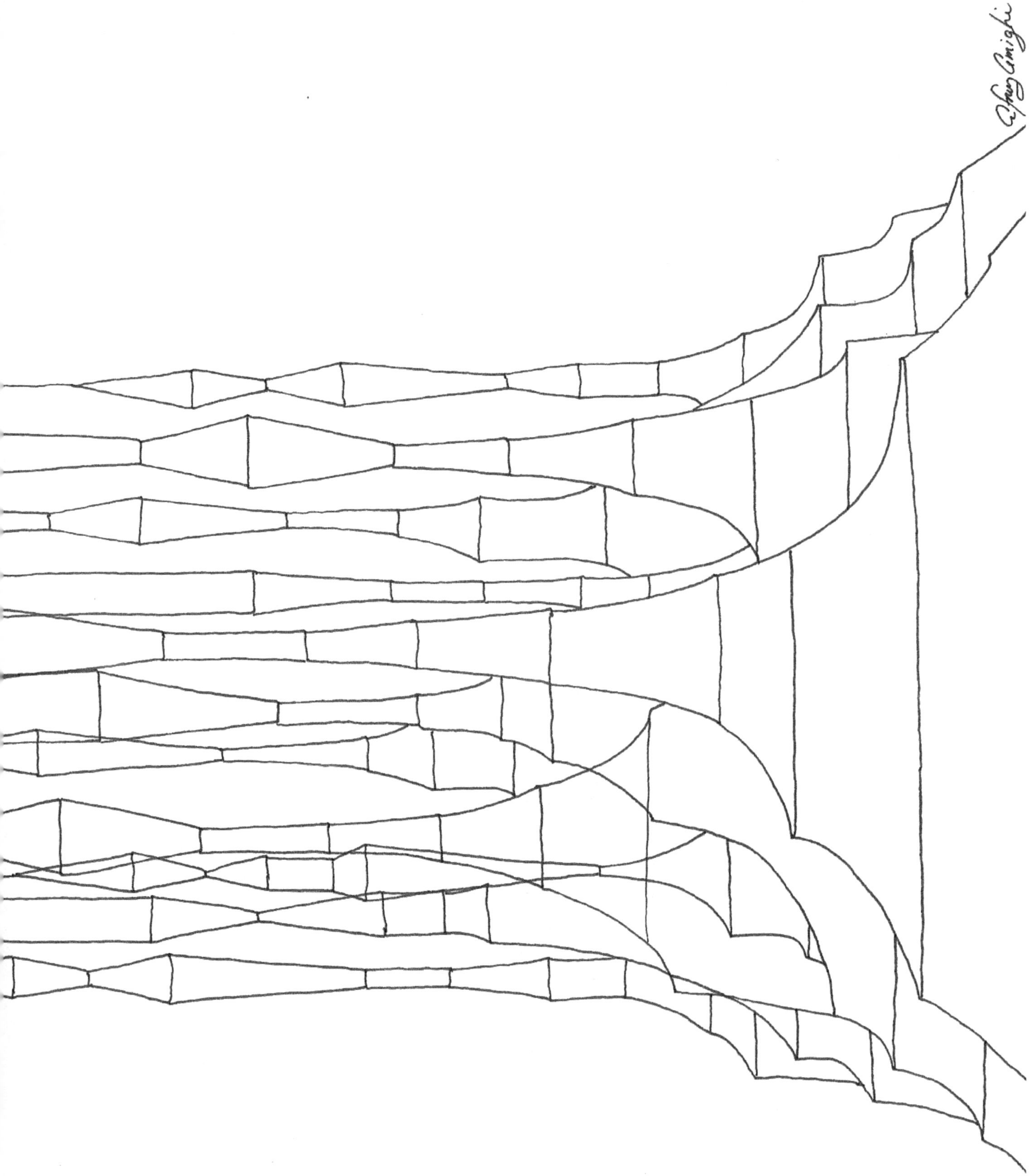

Andisheh Avini

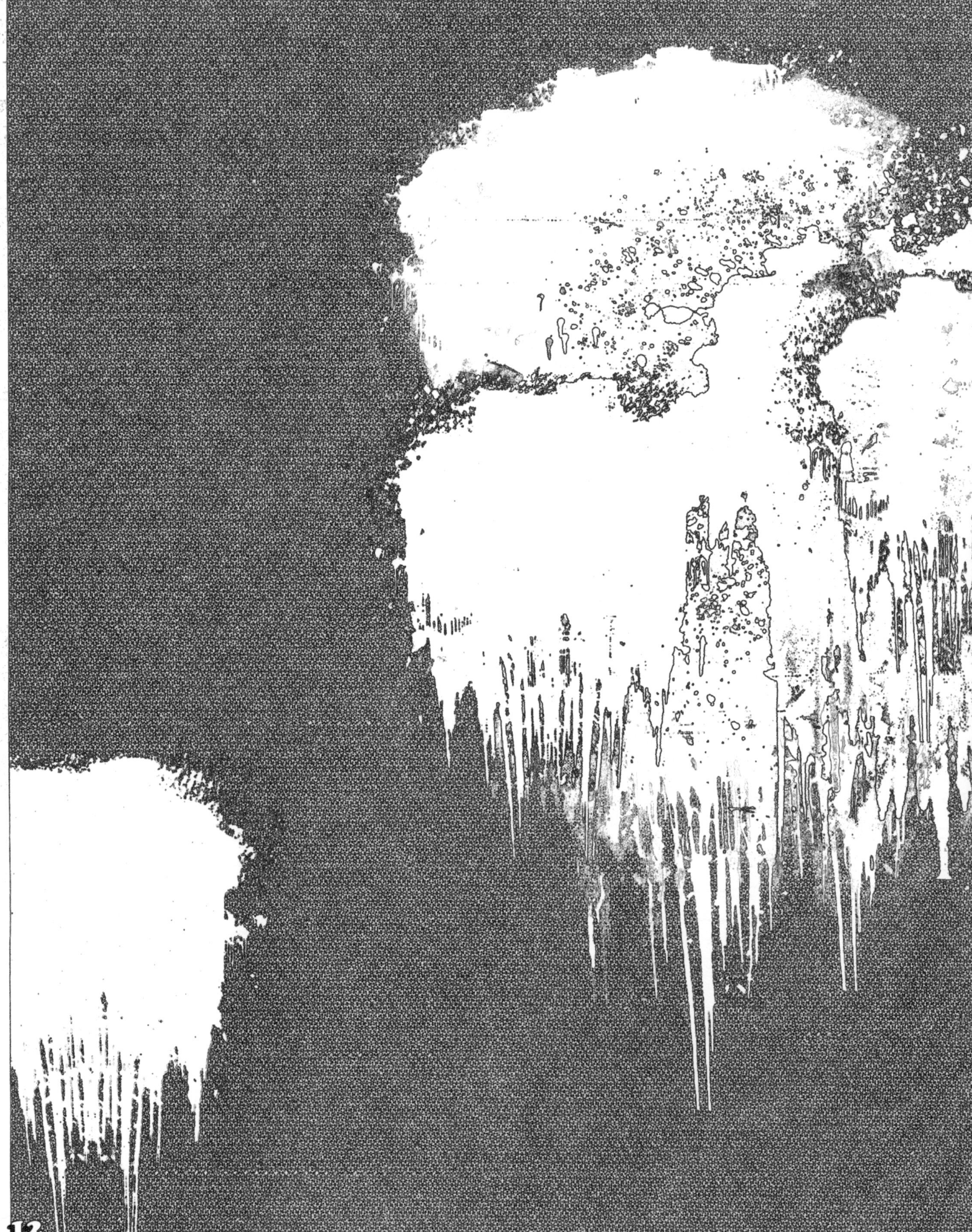

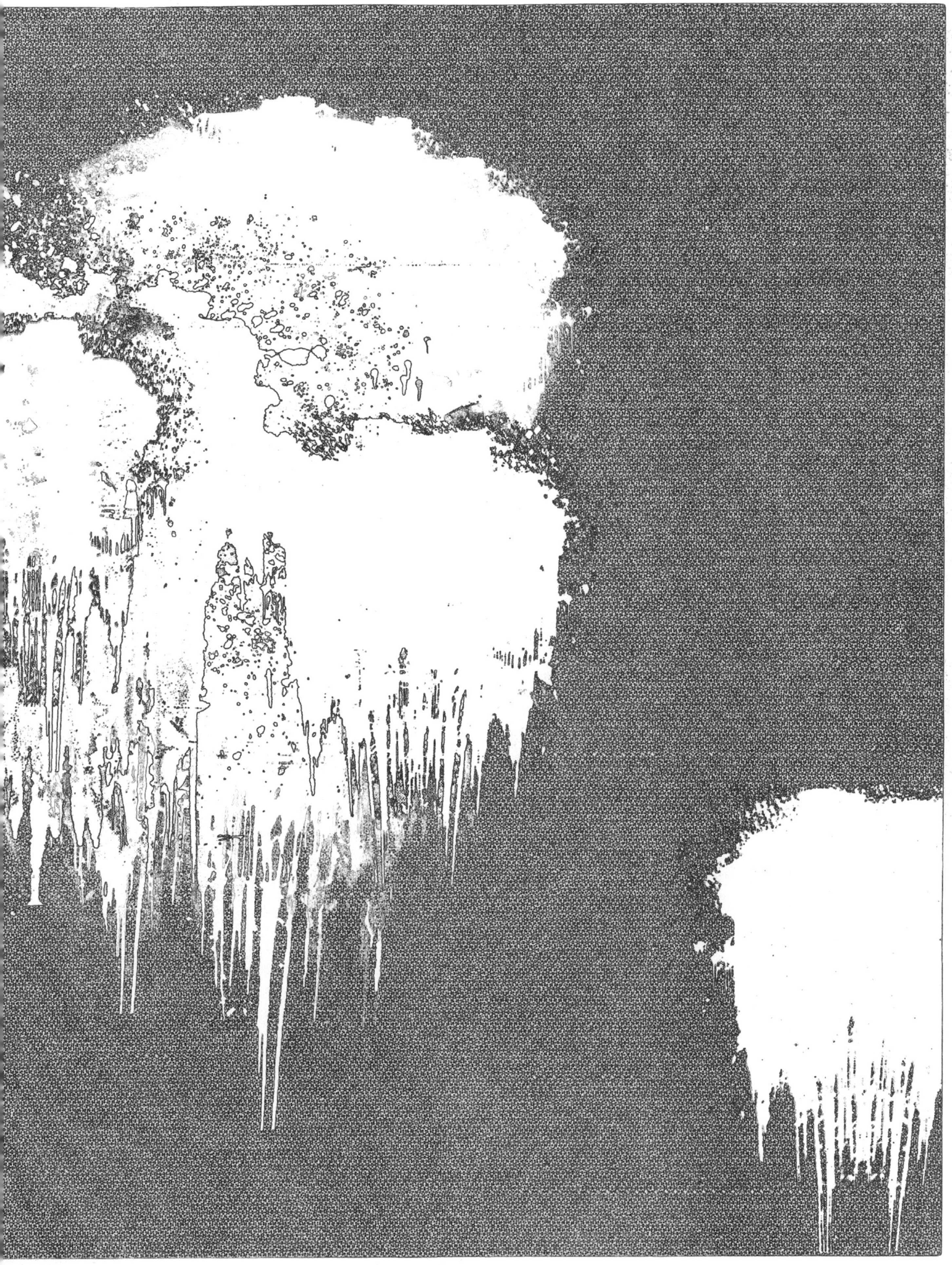

John Baldessari

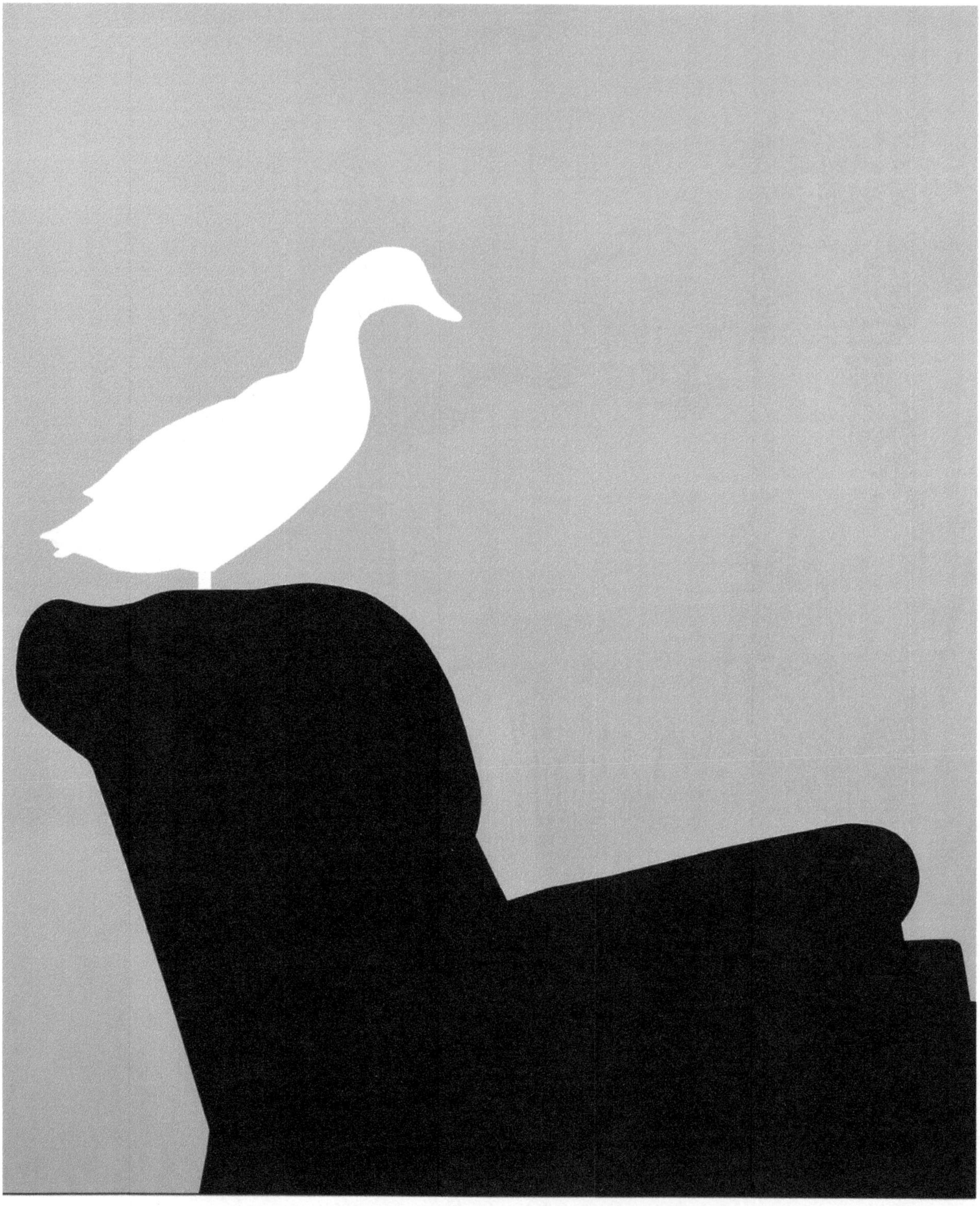

DUCK AND CHAIR

John Baldessari

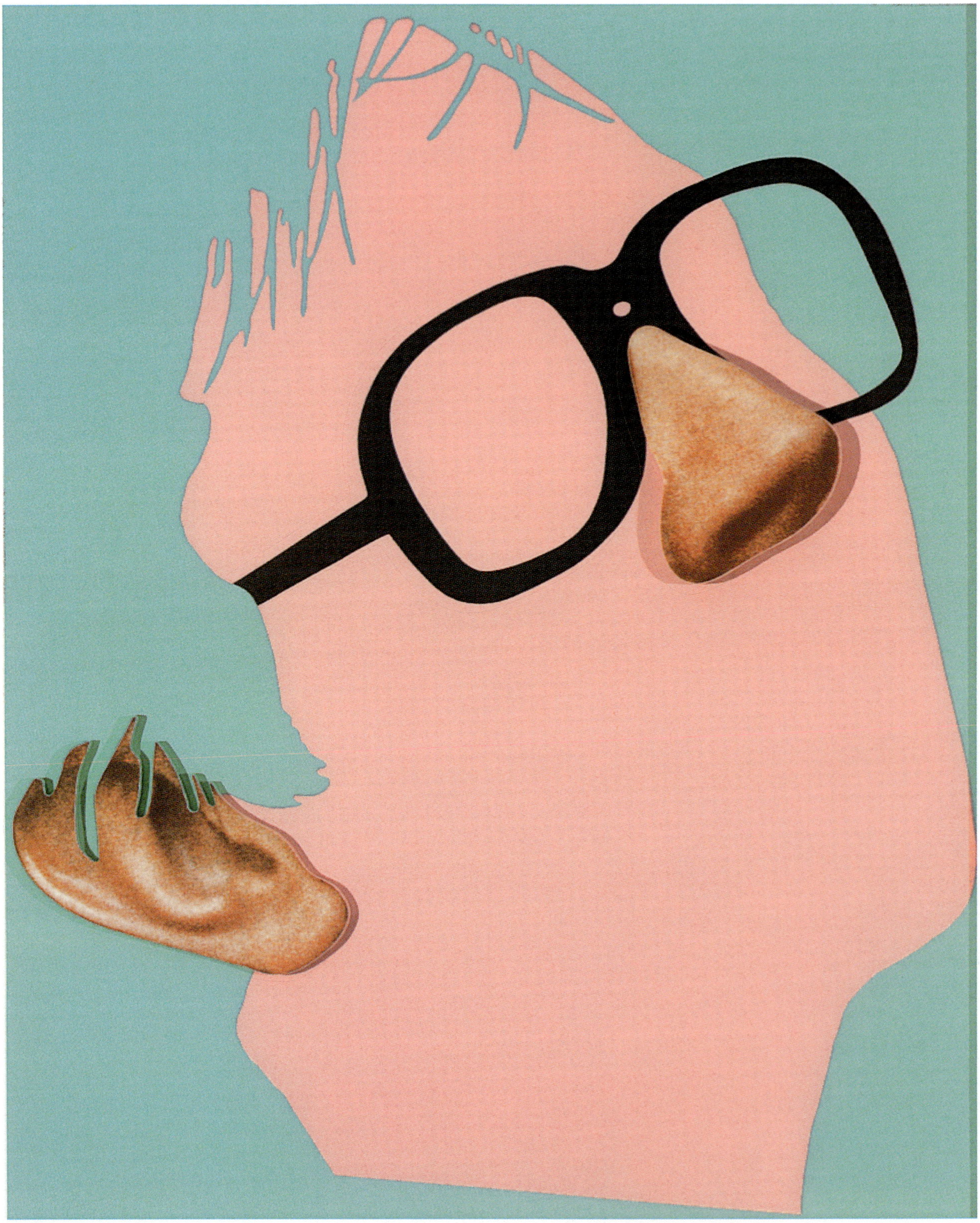

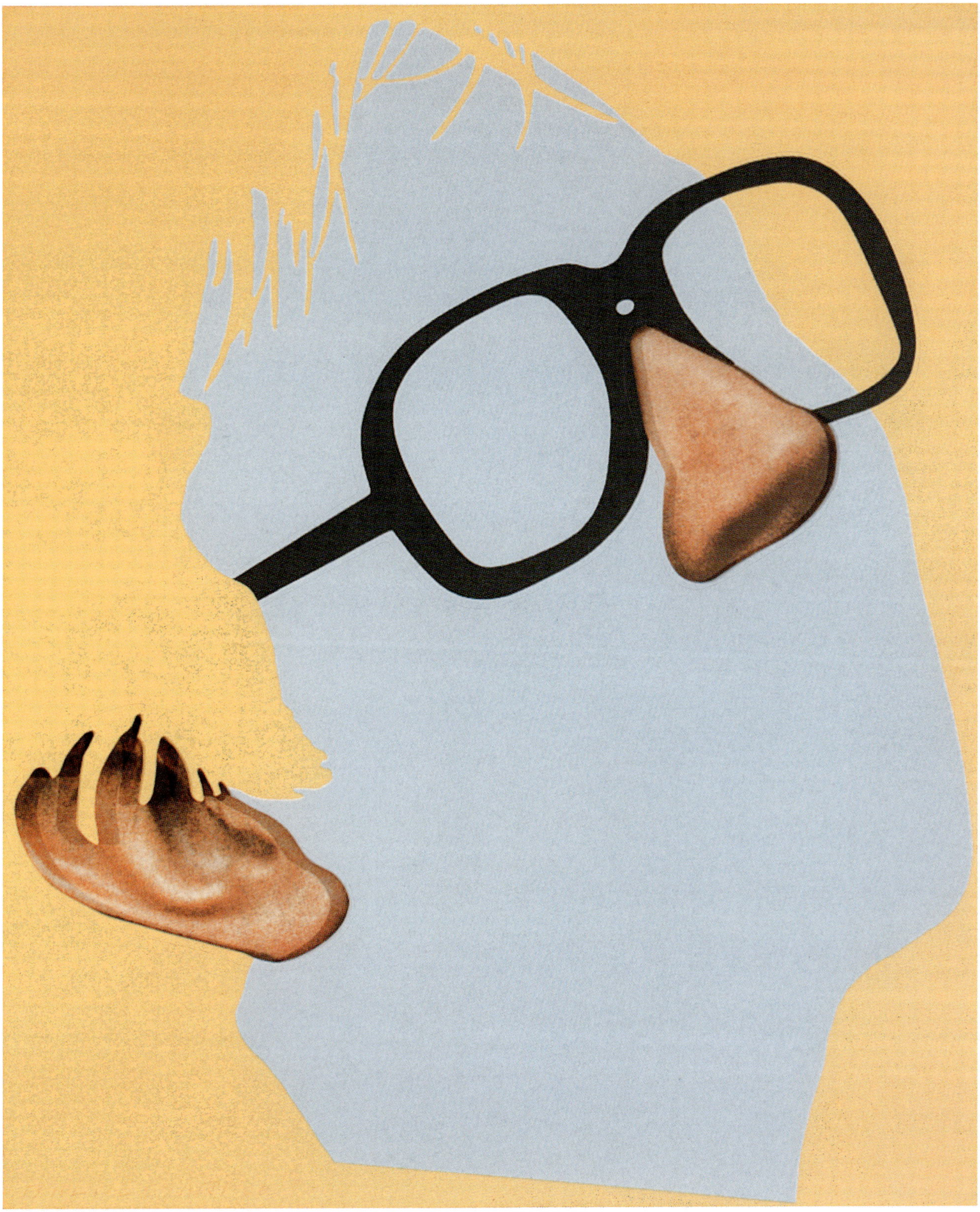

John Baldessari

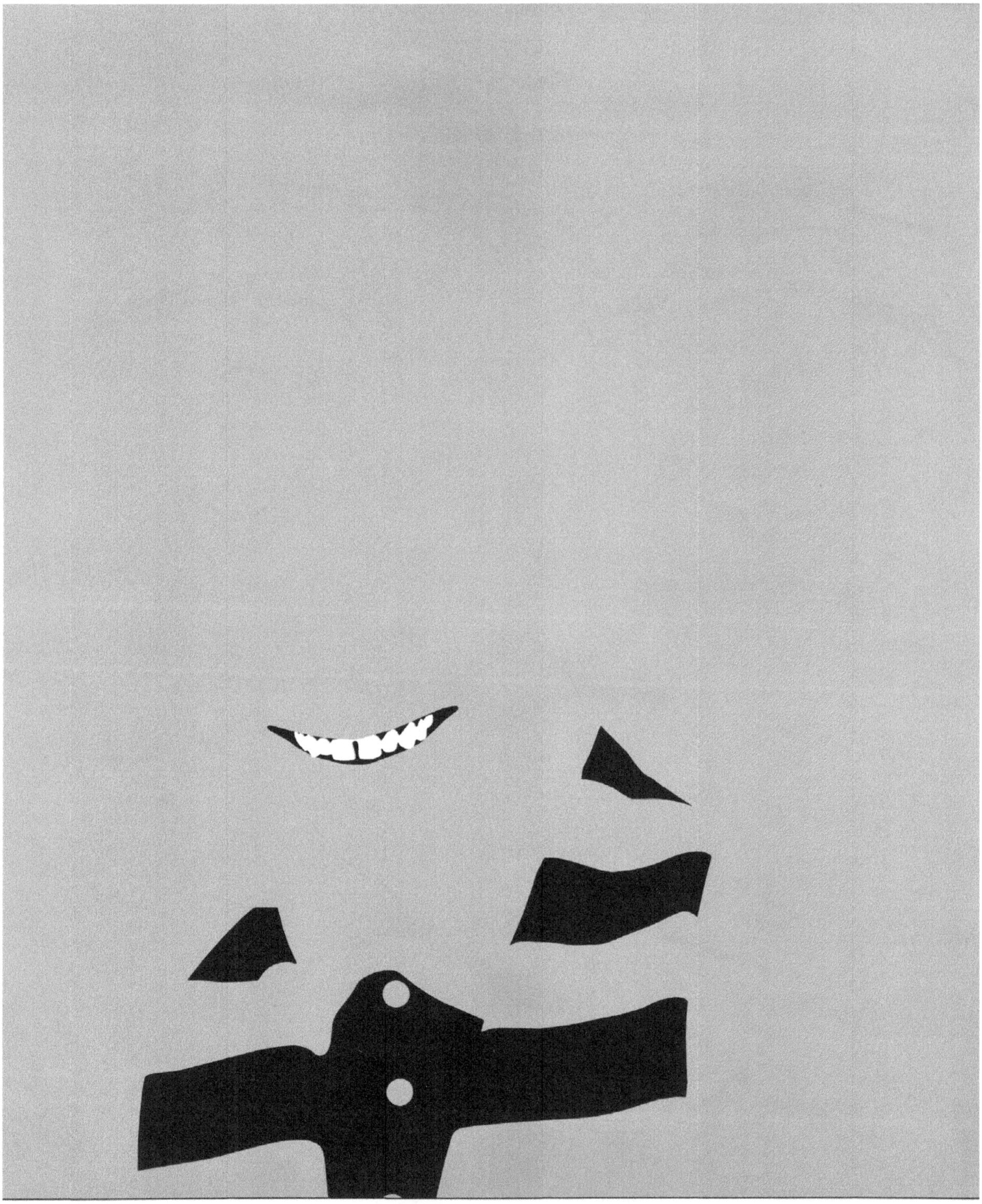

ELTON JOHN'S SMILE AND PORTION OF SHIRT

Barry X Ball

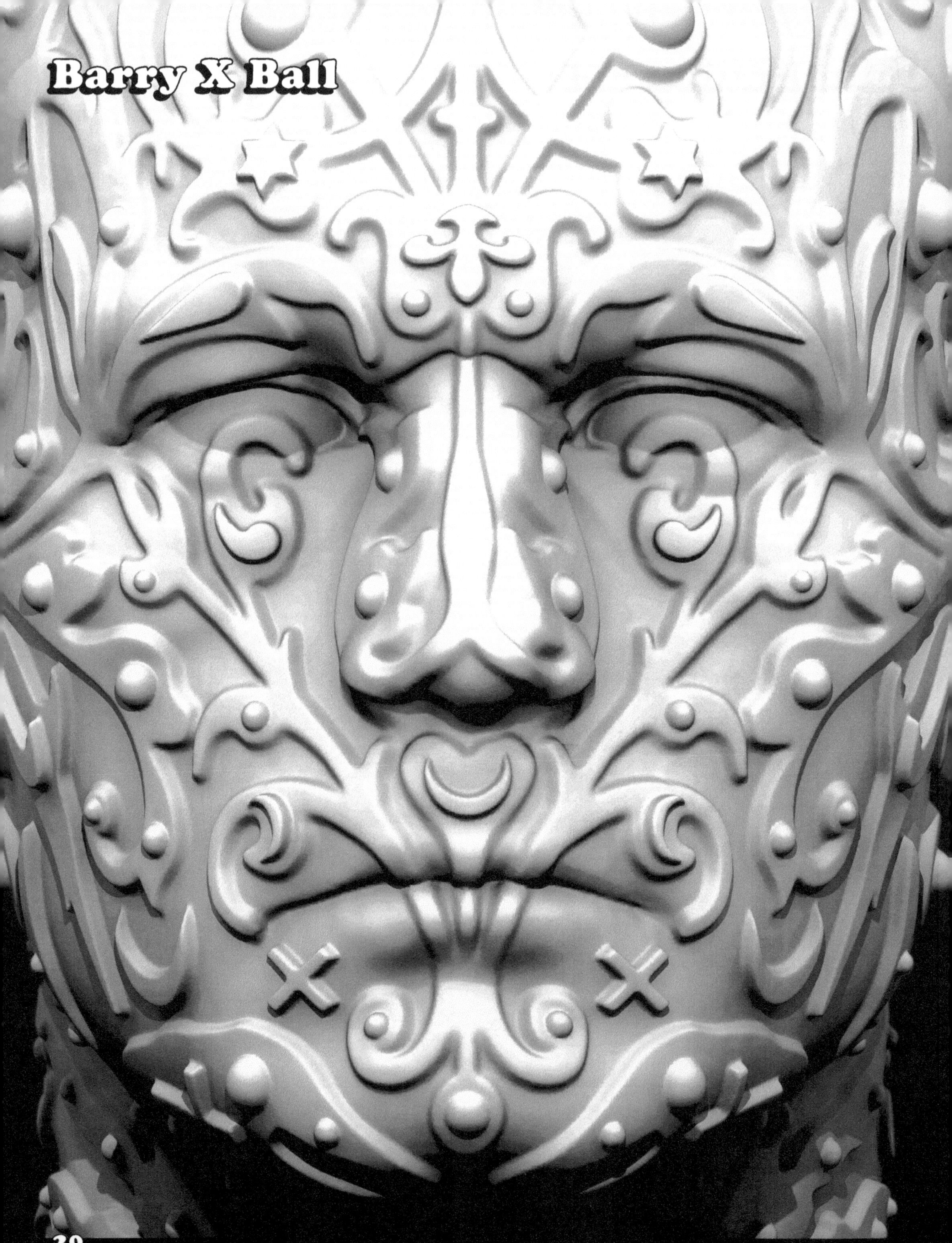

a meta-portrait pairing of the artist, screaming, and Matthew Barney, stoically becalmed, both richly embossed, in a manner

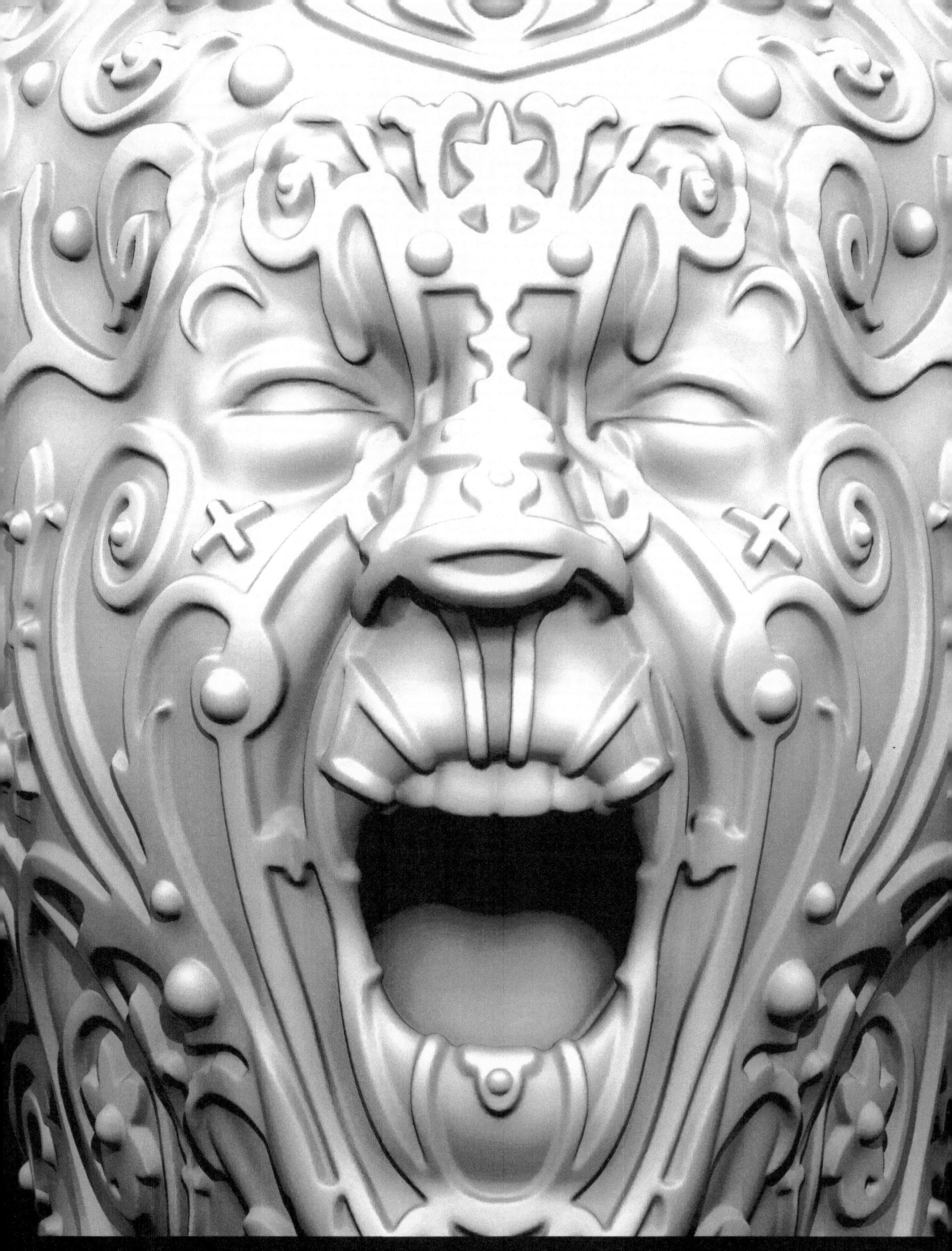

cent of late-Rennaisance Milanese parade armor, with a cornucopia of silhoutted motifs and protuberant, warty, half spheres.

Ali Banisadr

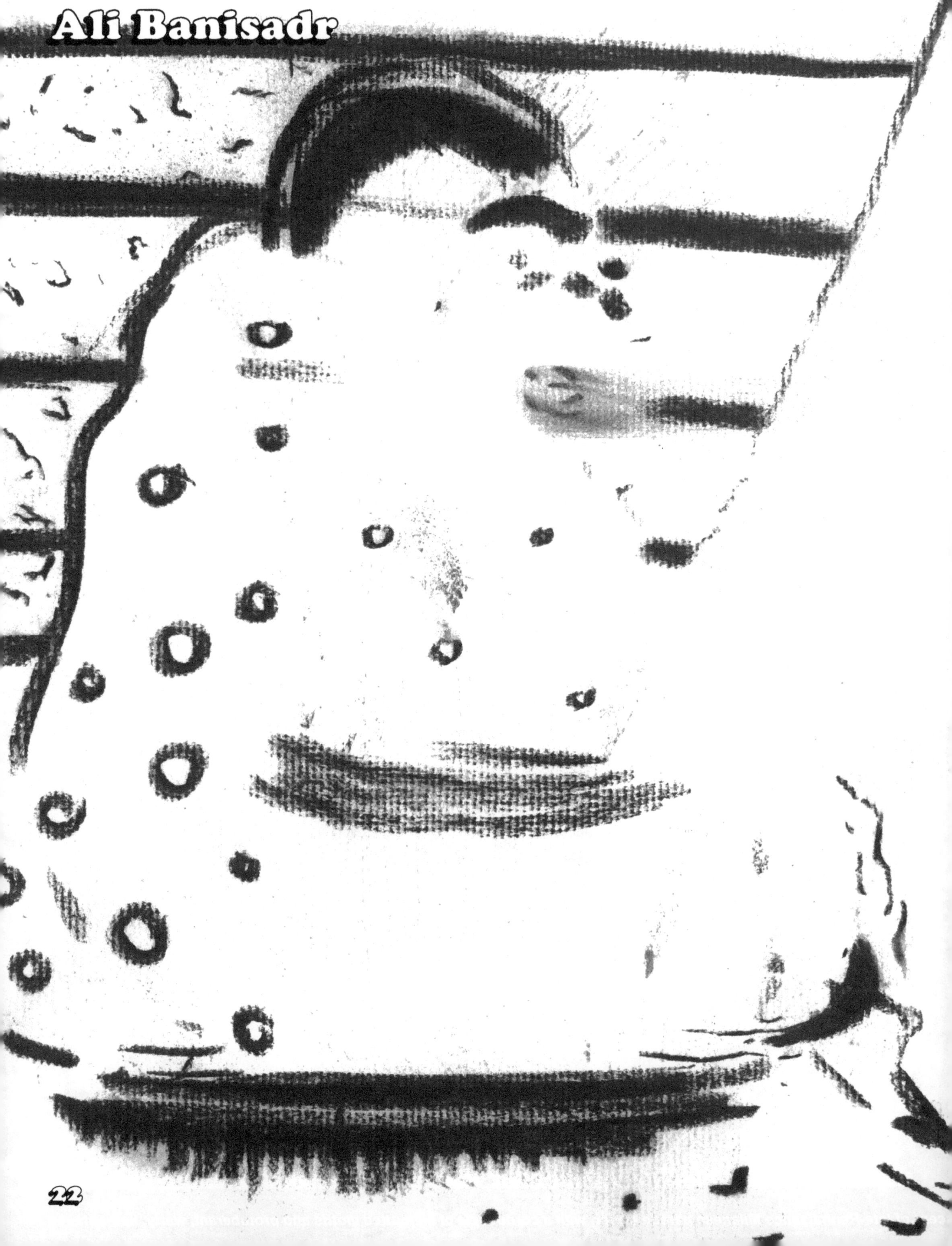

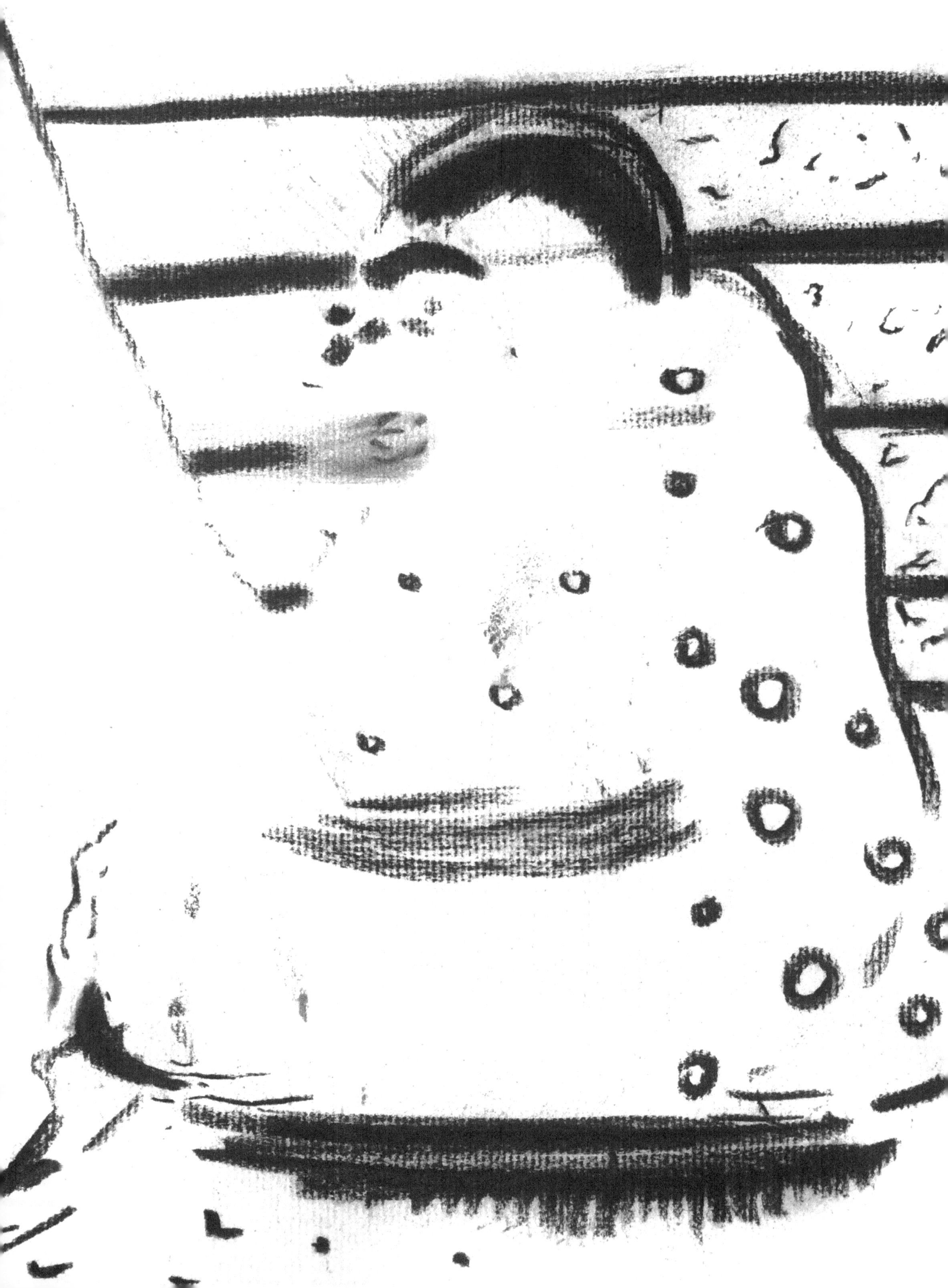

Phyllida Barlow

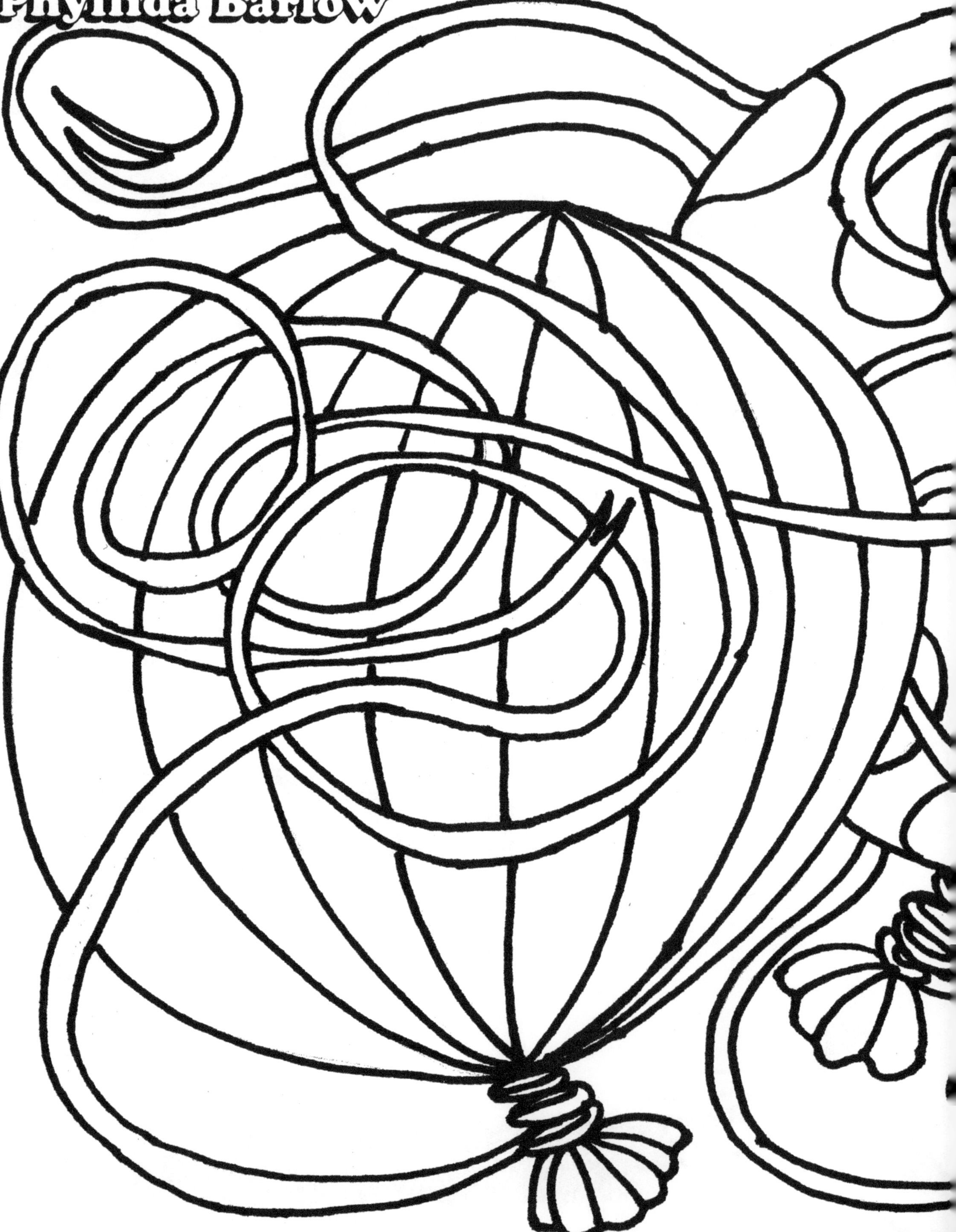

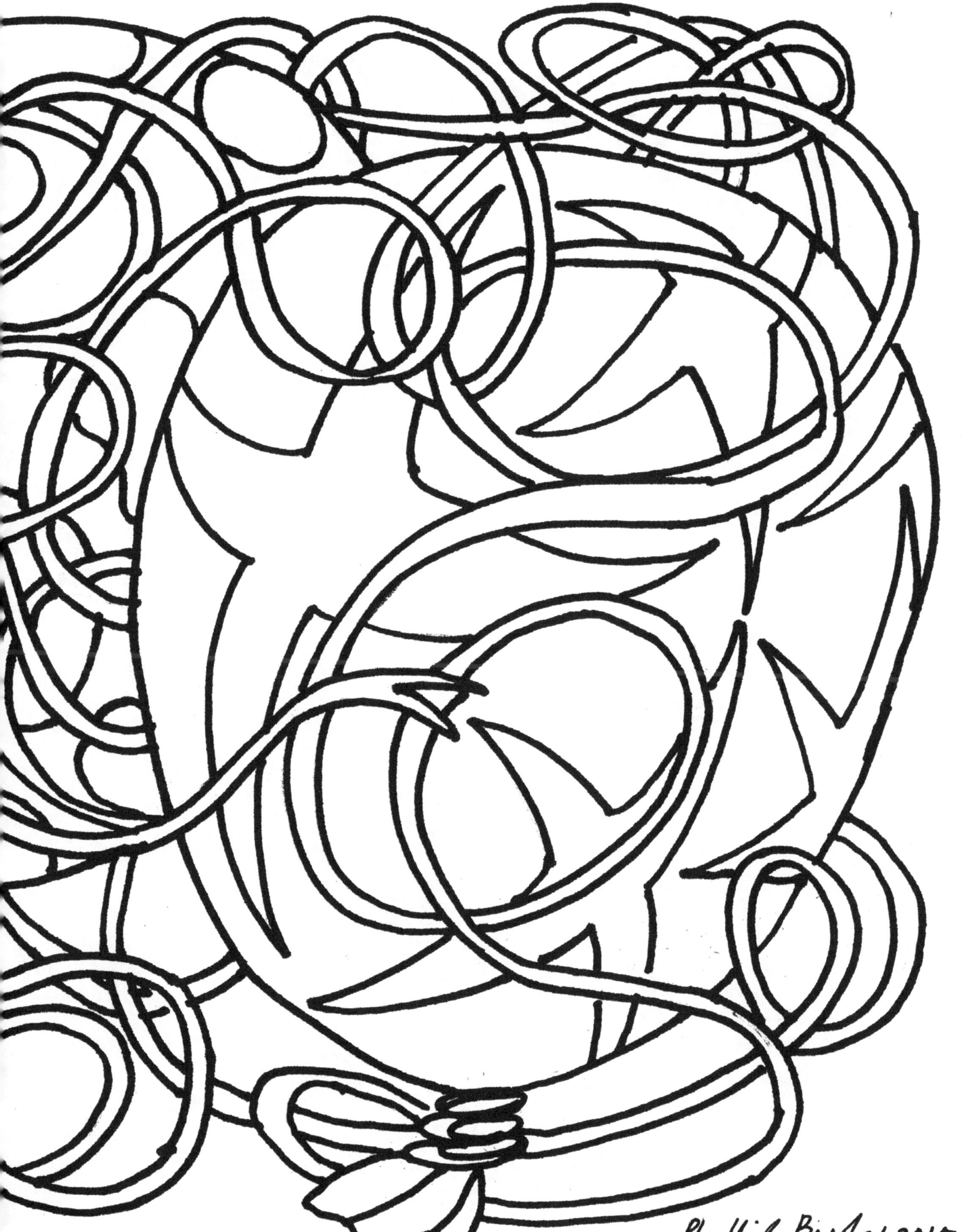

Phyllida Barlow 2015

Sanford Biggers

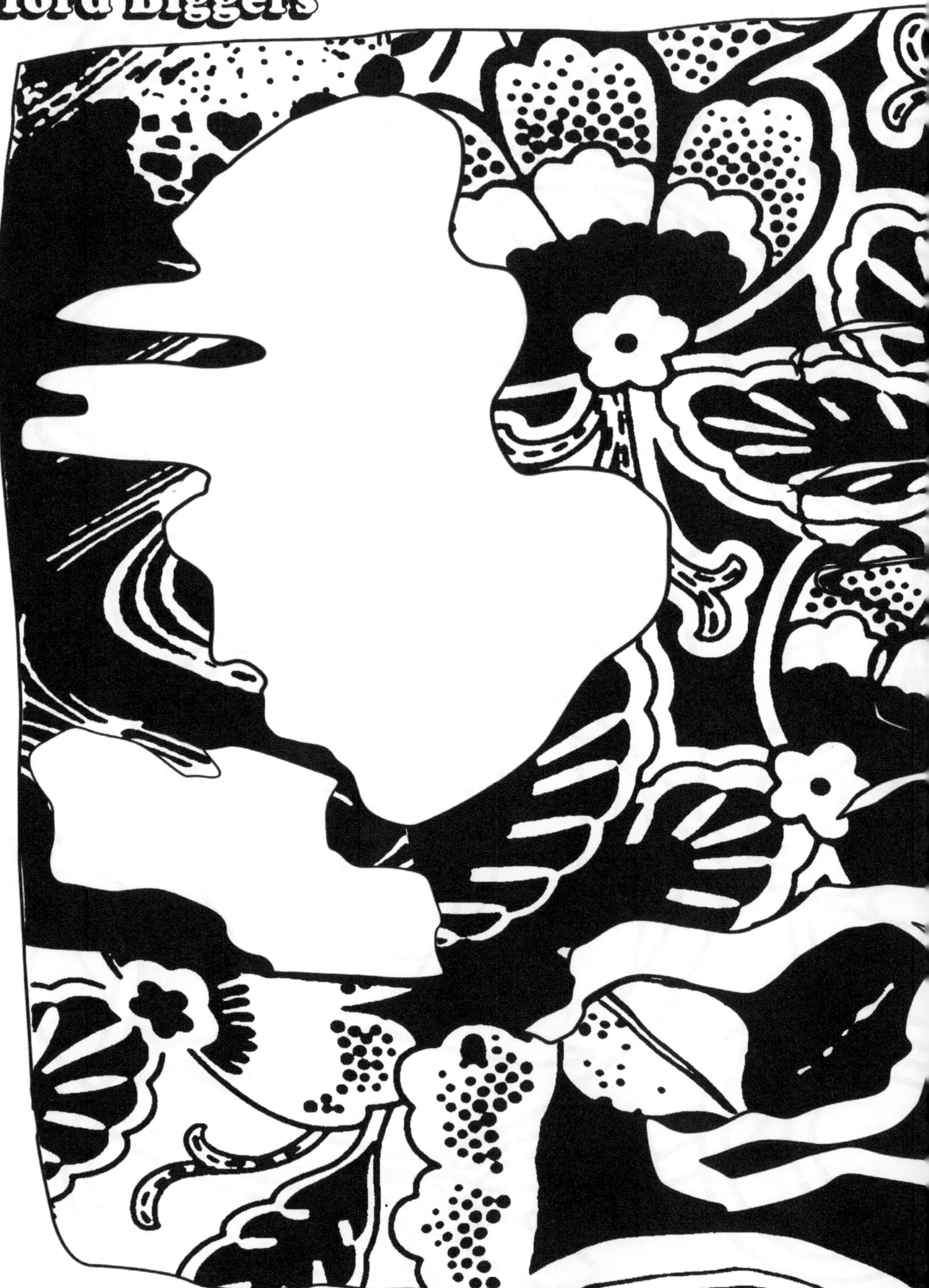

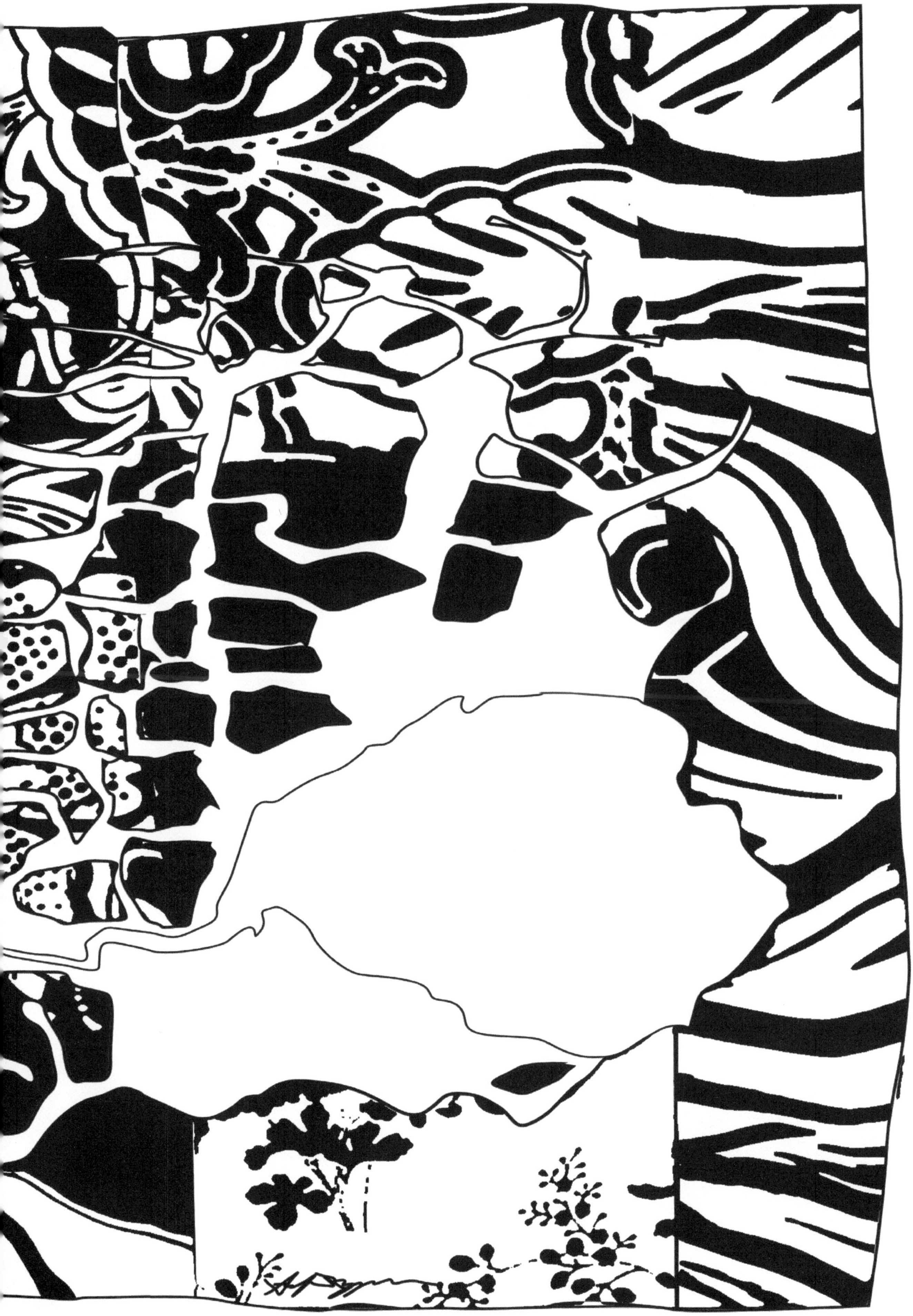

Olaf Breuning

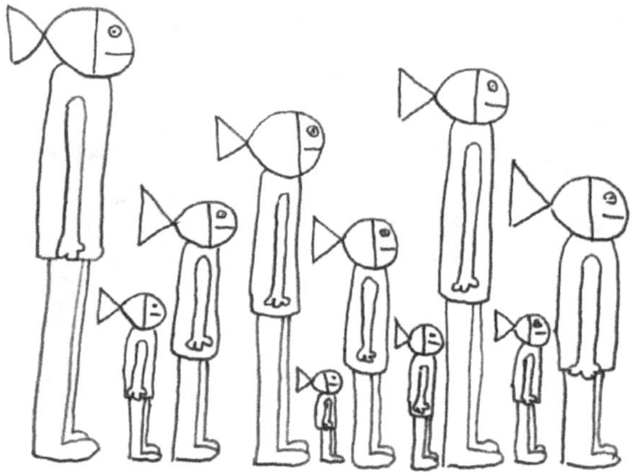

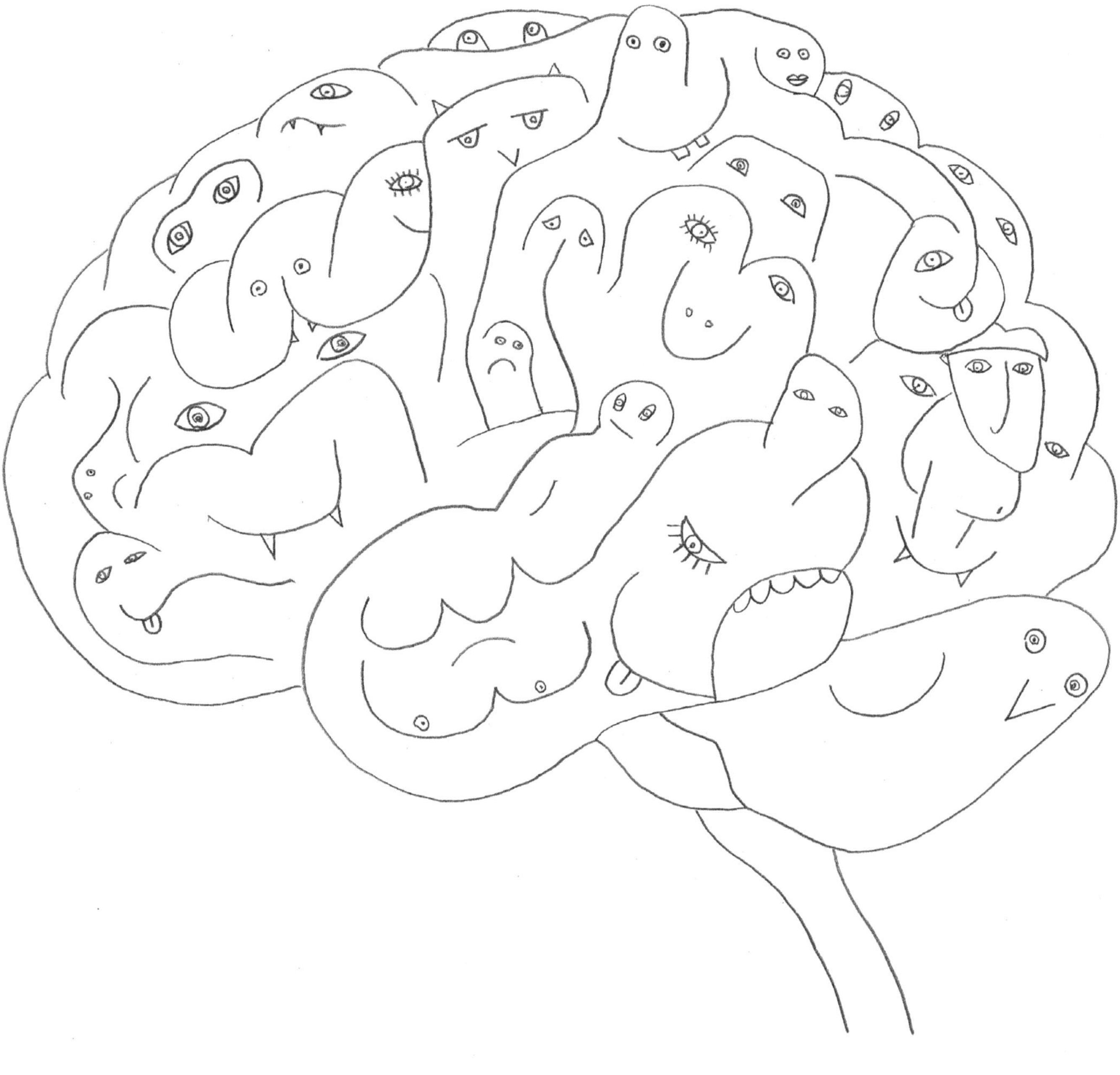

Rebecca Chamberlain

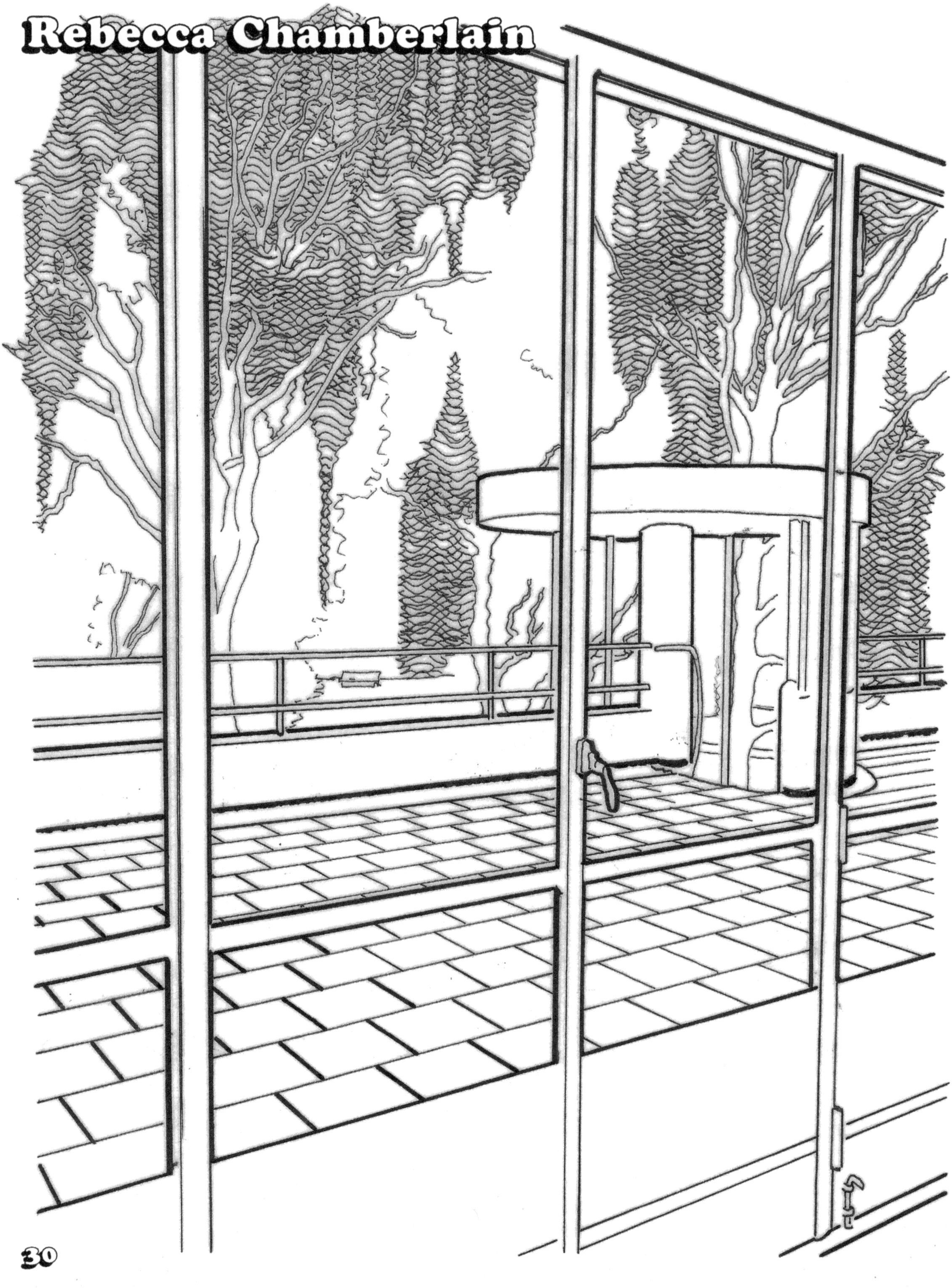

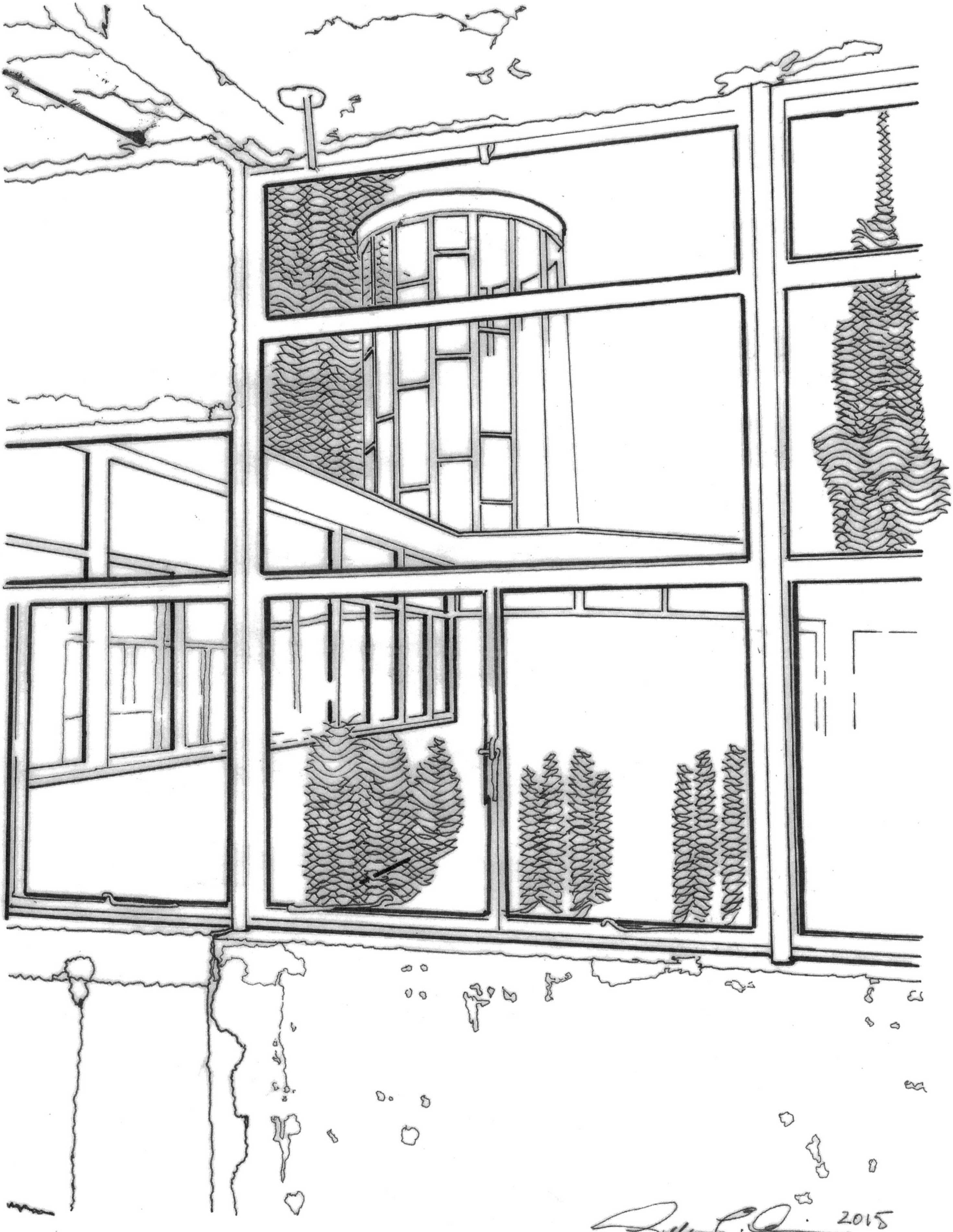
2015

Julia Chiang

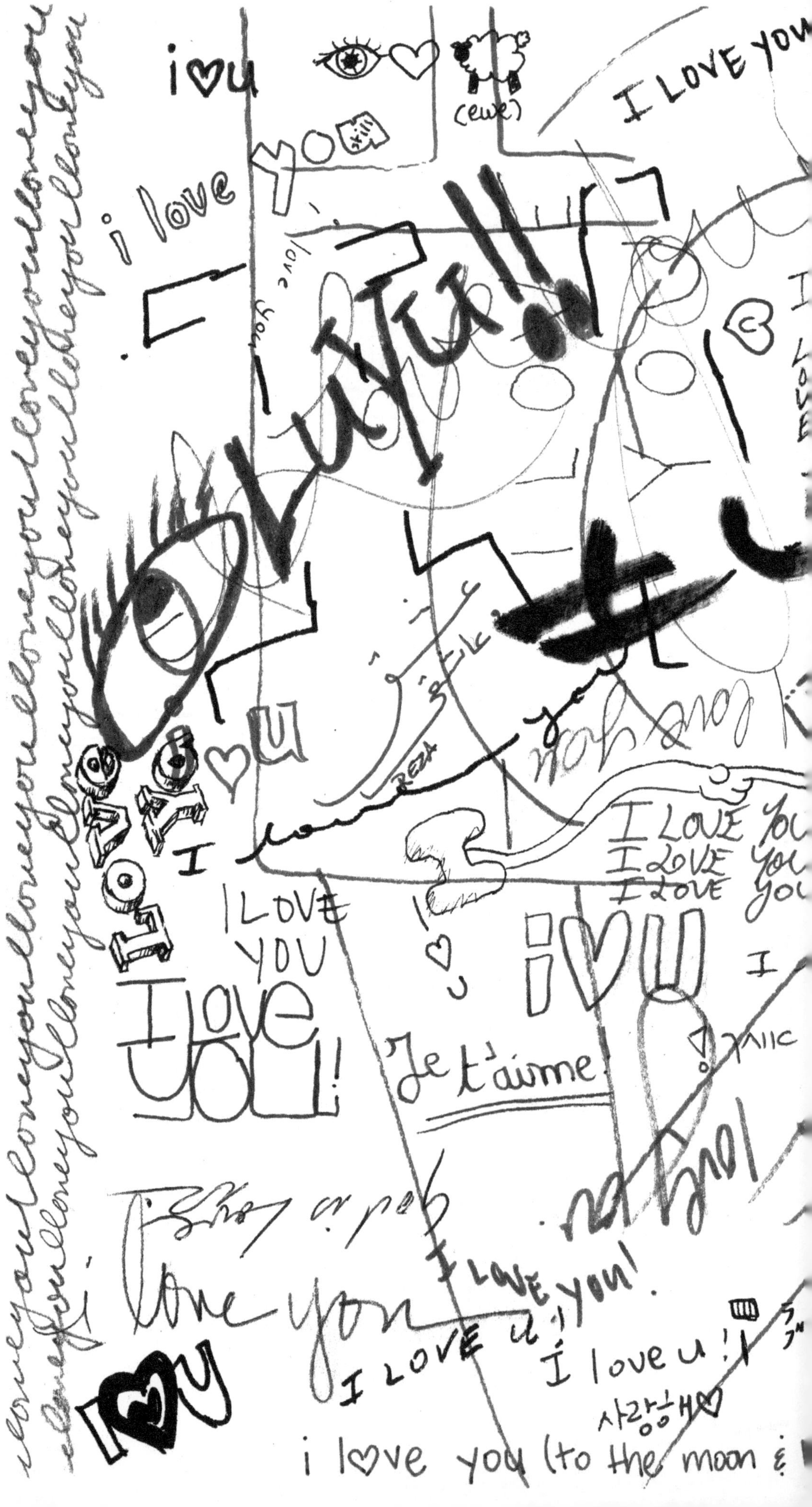

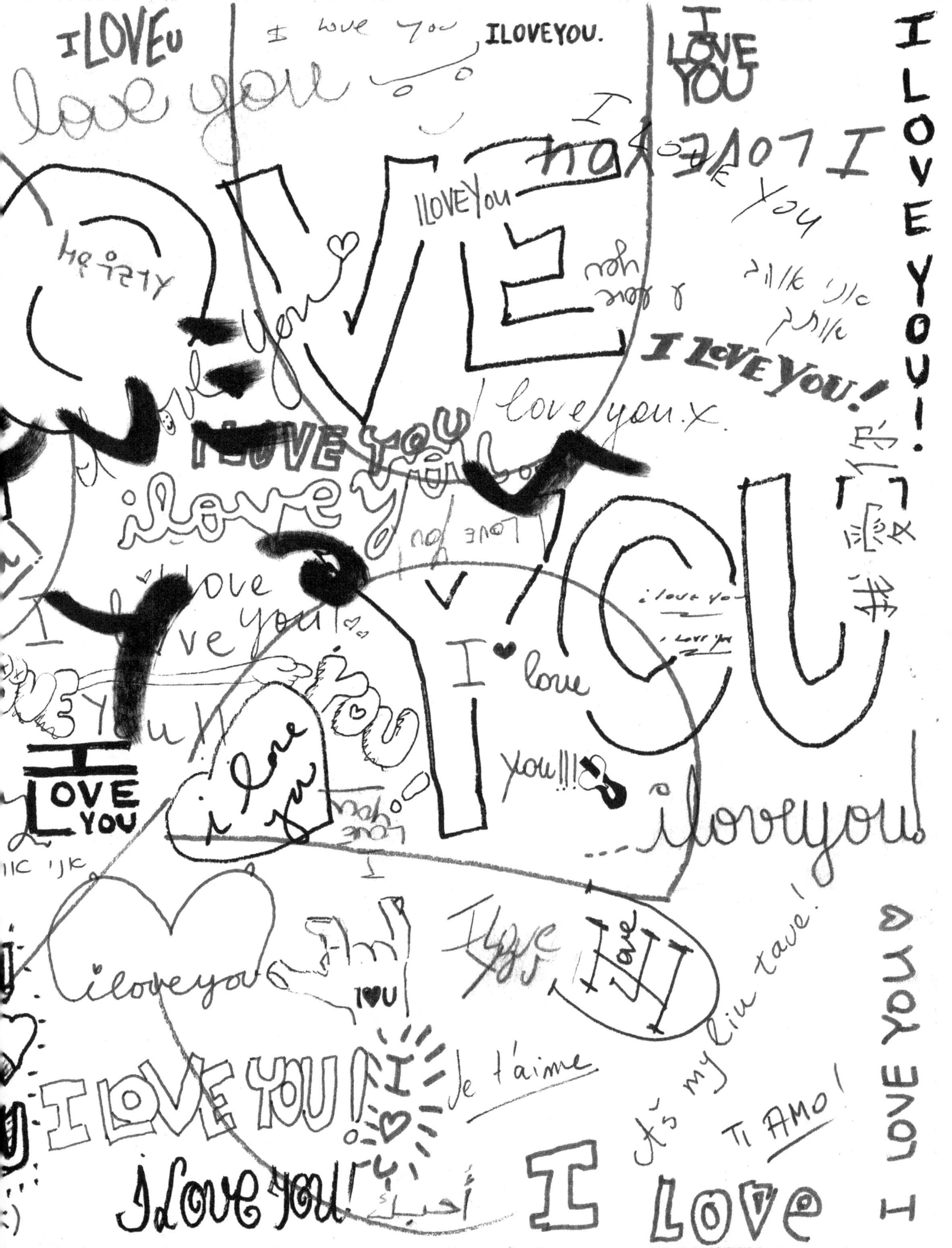

I LOVEU
I love you
ILOVEYOU.
I LOVE YOU
I LOVE YOU!
love you
ILOVEYou
I LOVE YOU!
I love you. x
I LOVE YOU
i love you
I love you
I love
you!!!
iloveyou!
I LOVE YOU
iloveyou
I♥U
I love
I LOVE YOU!
Je t'aime
It's my liu tave!
TI AMO!
I love YOU!
I Love
I LOVE YOU♥

Will Cotton

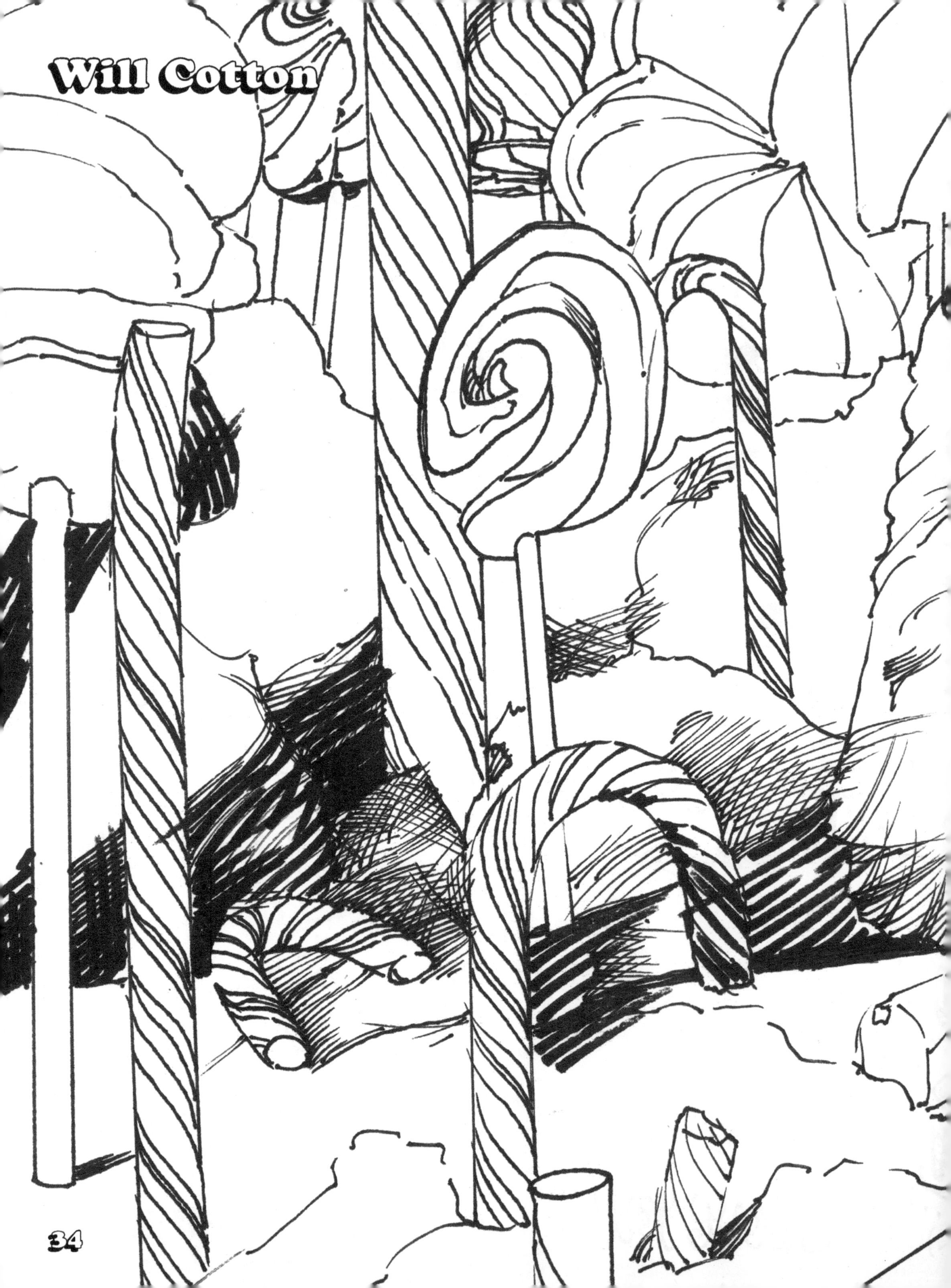

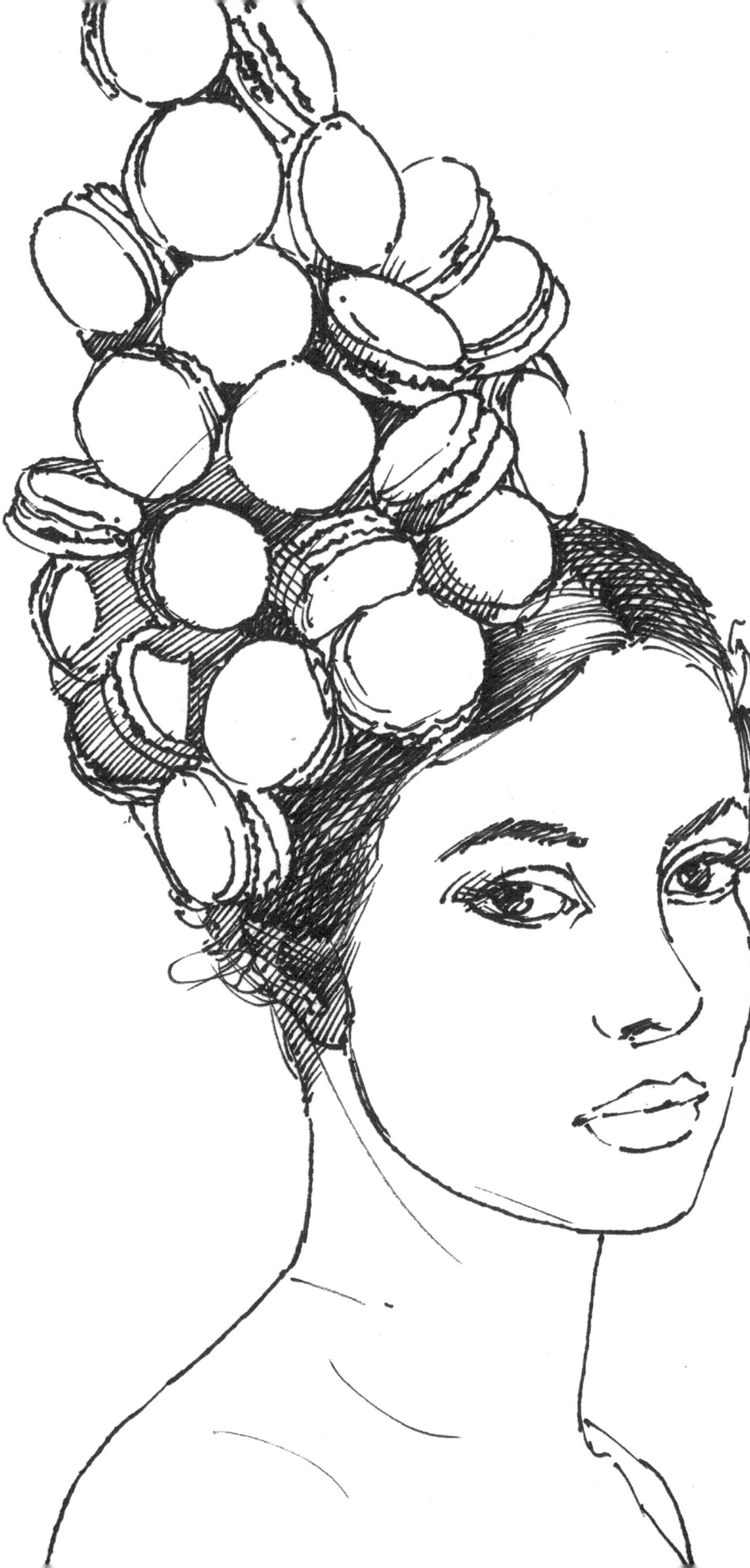

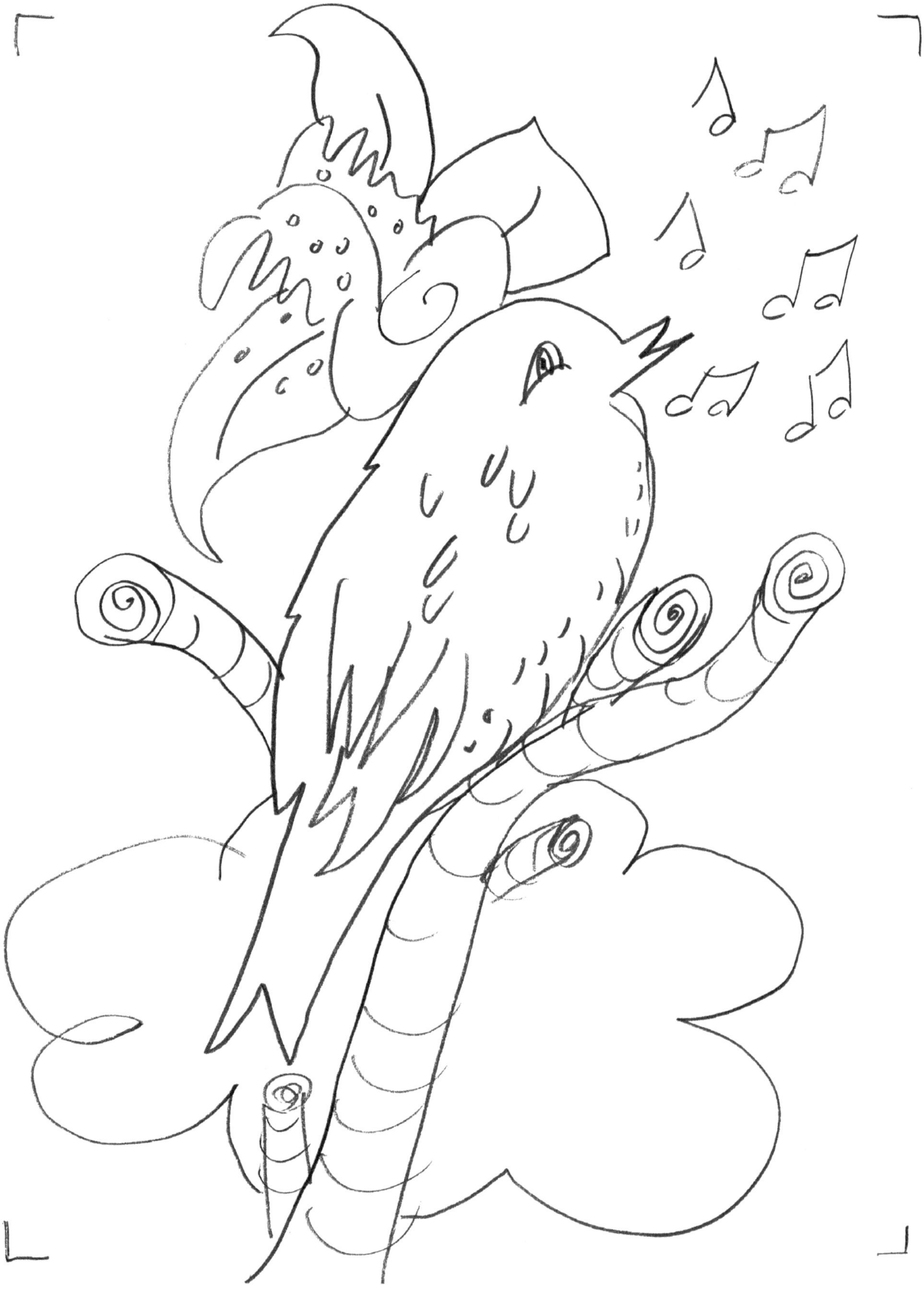

Aaron Curry

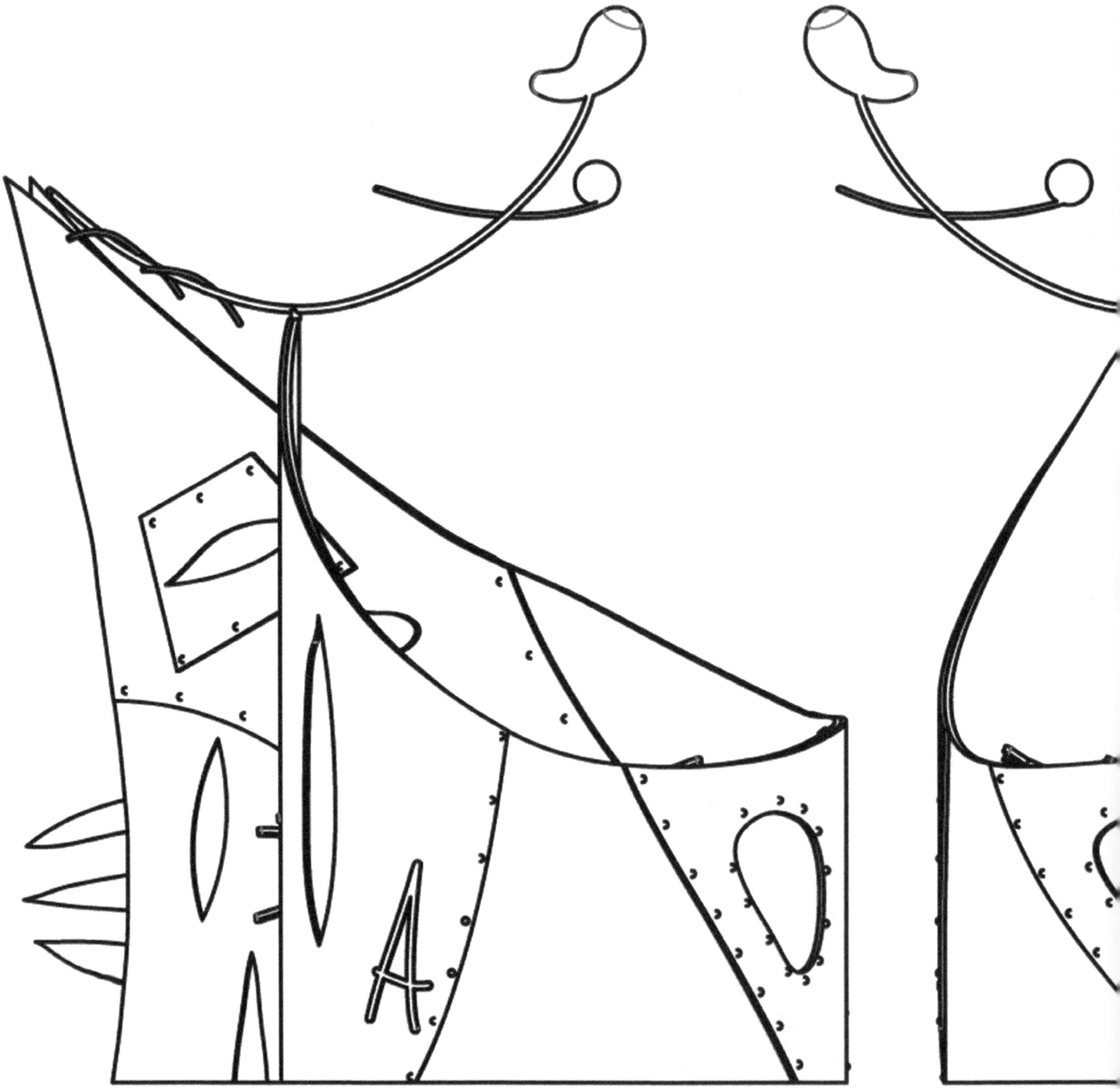

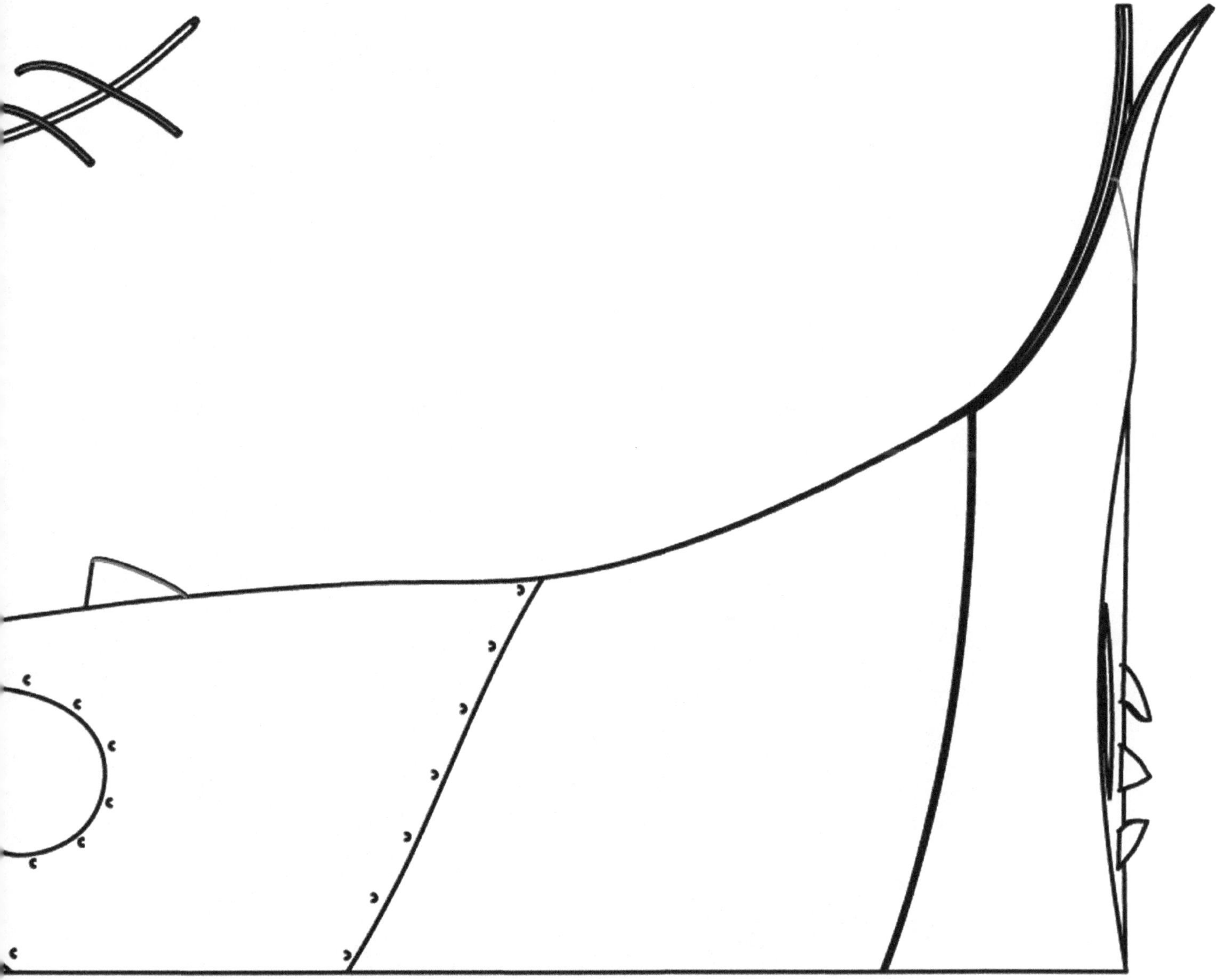

N. Dash

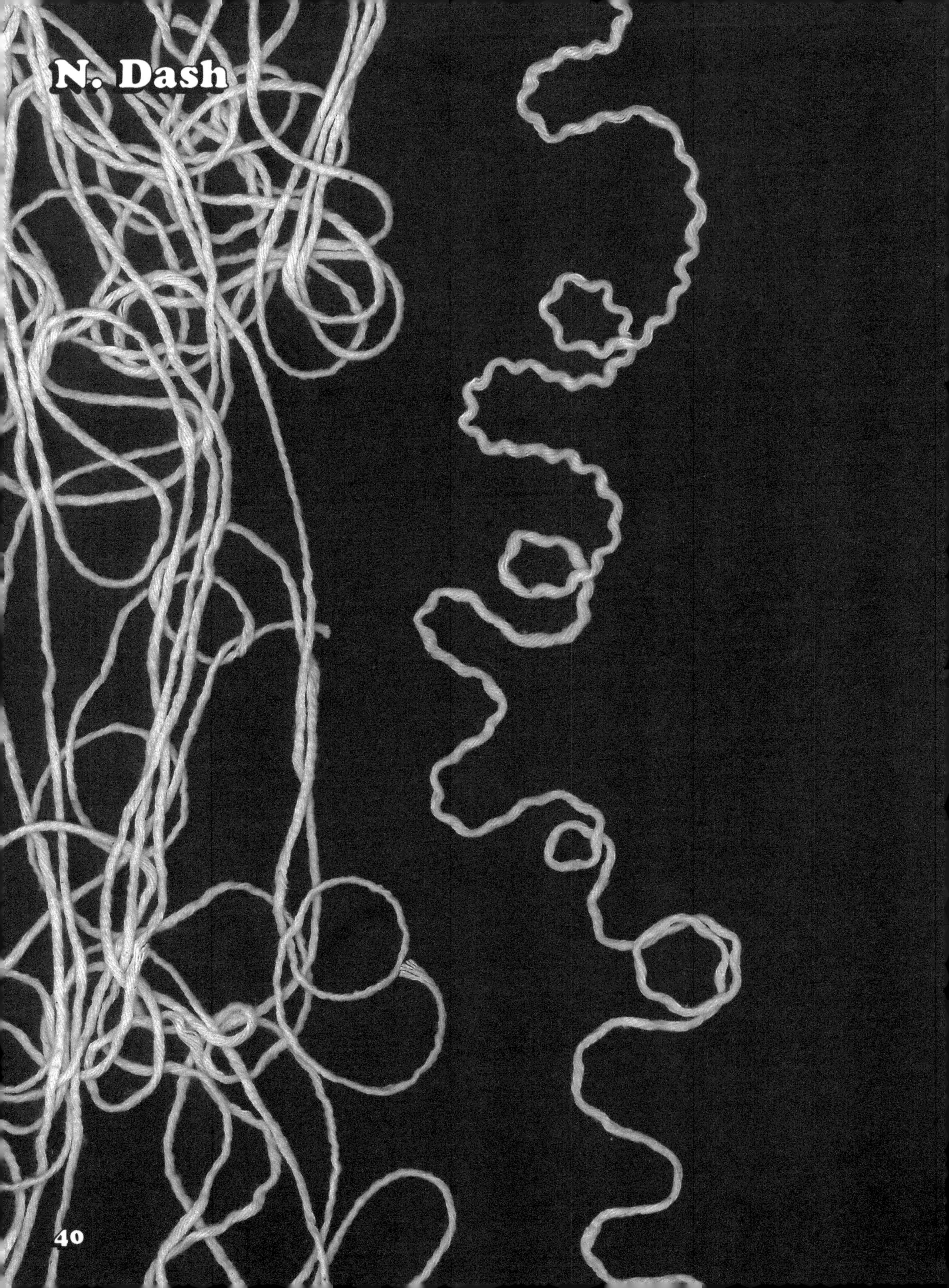

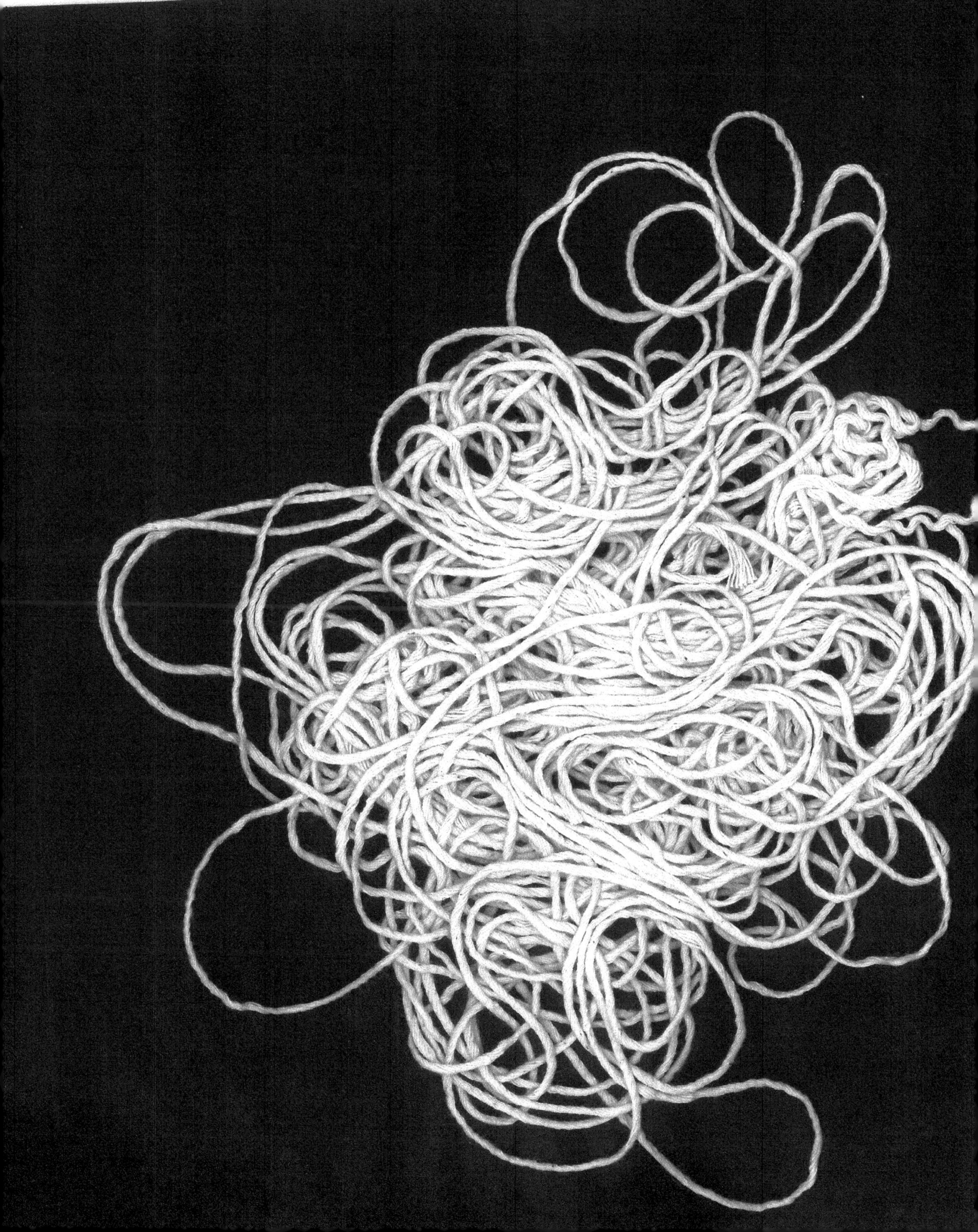

Wim Delvoye

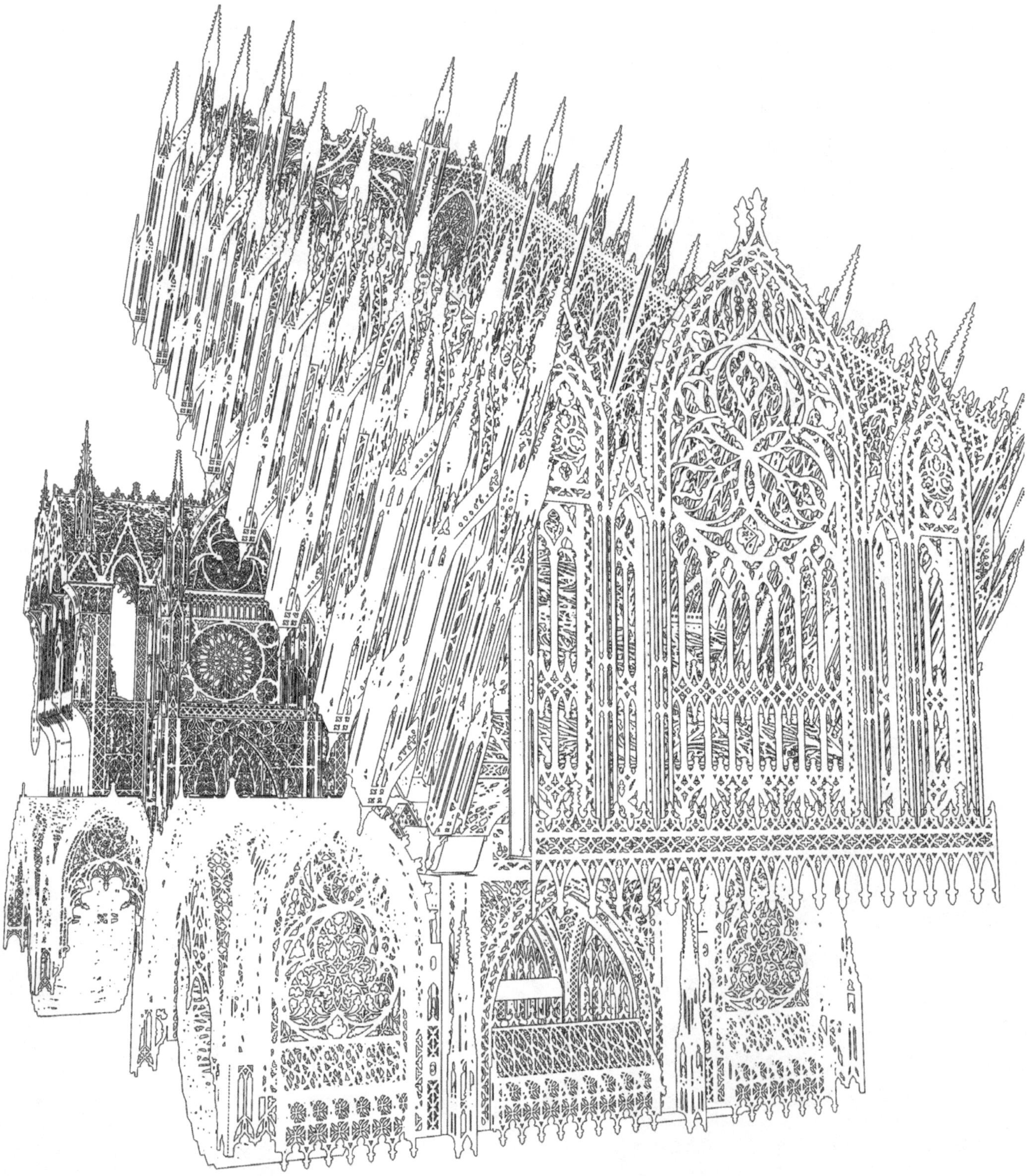

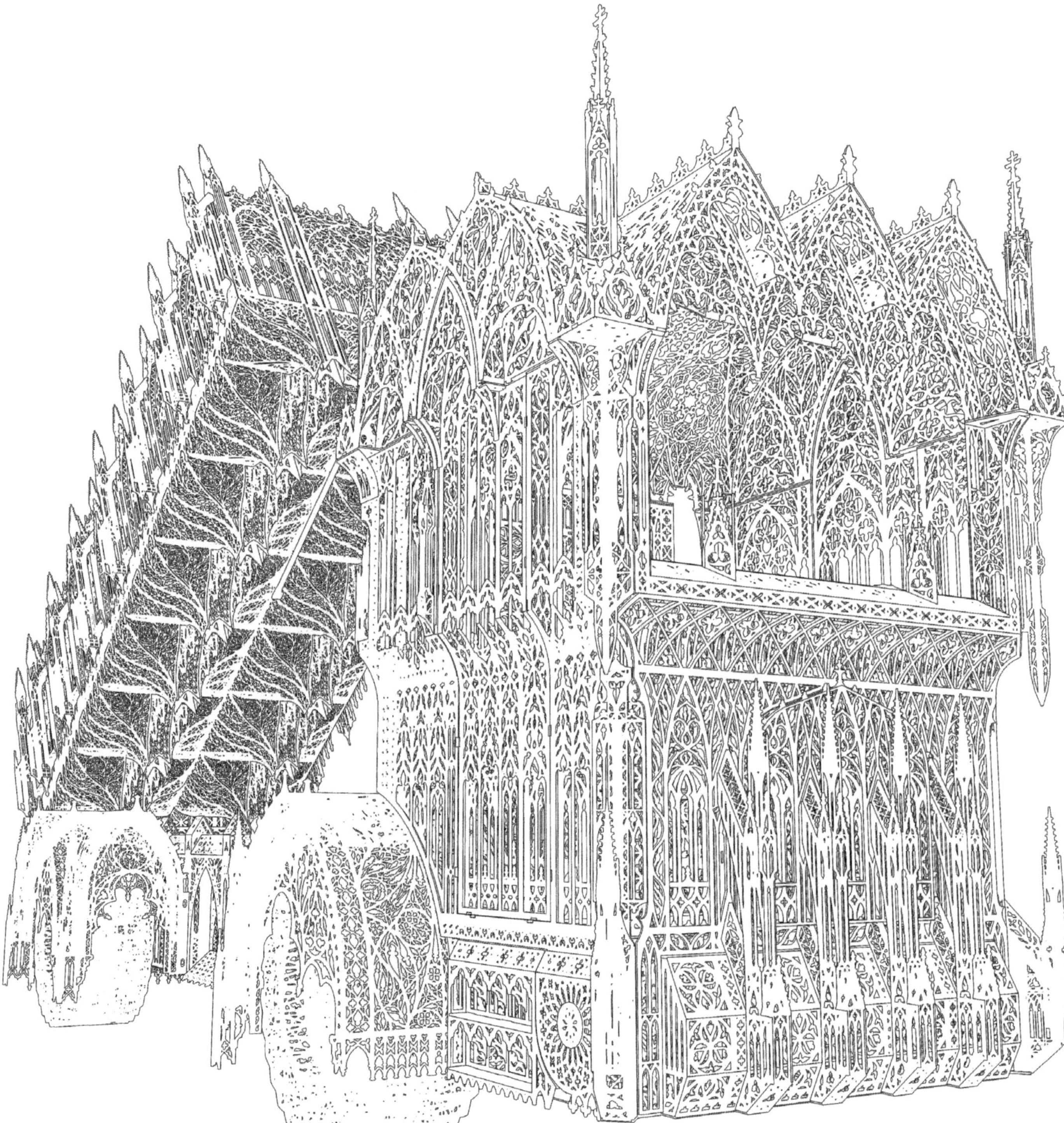

Claudia DeMonte

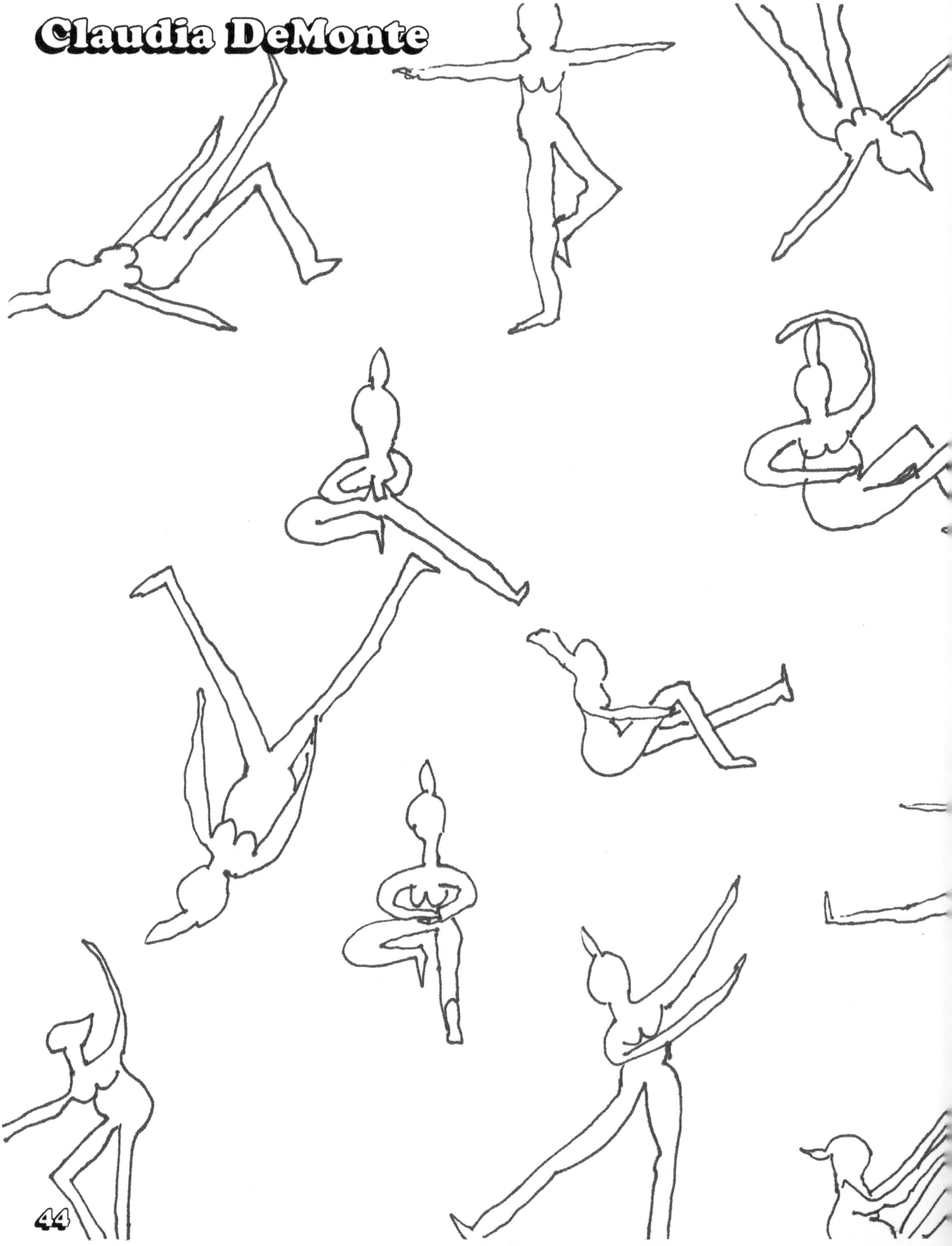

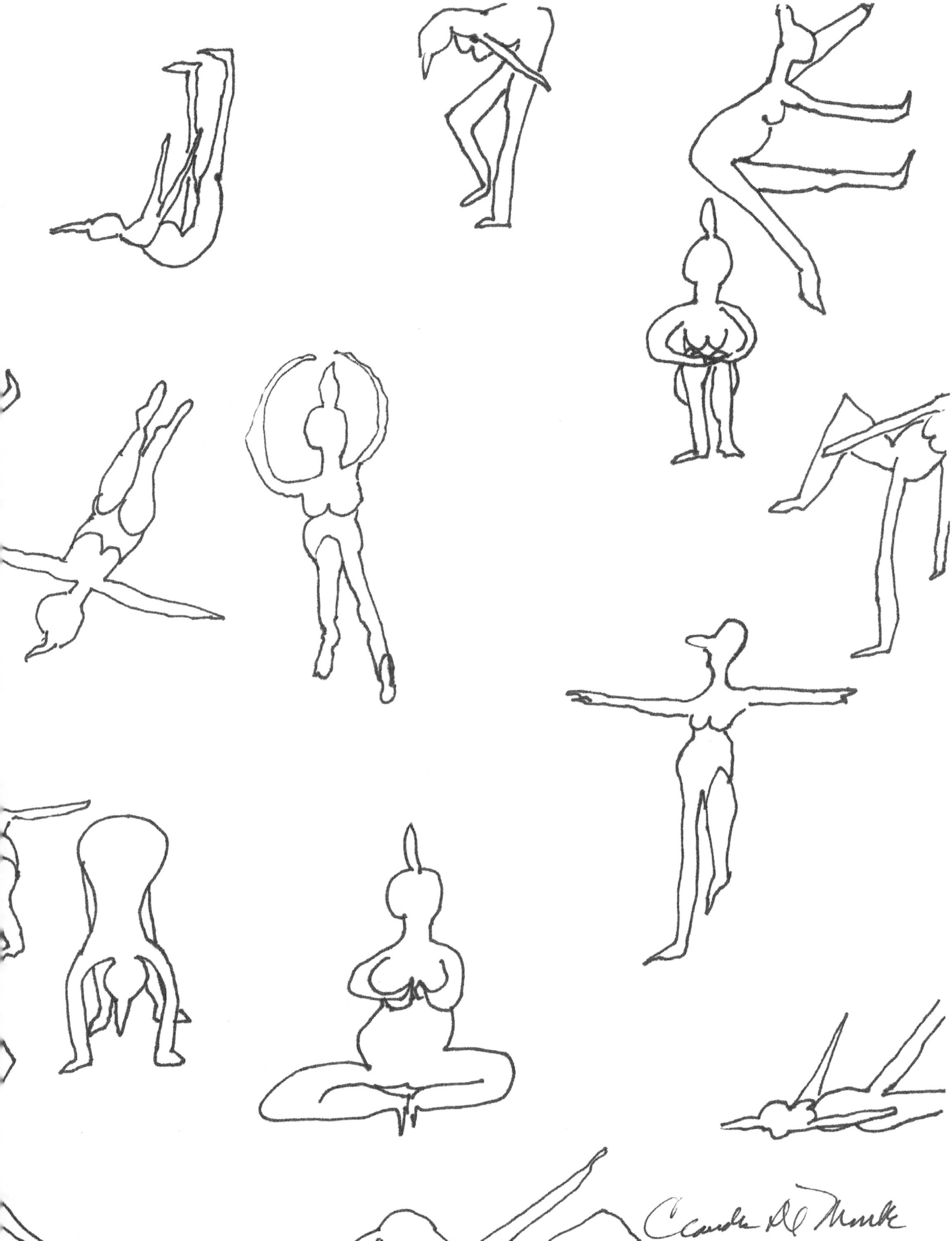

Kim Dingle

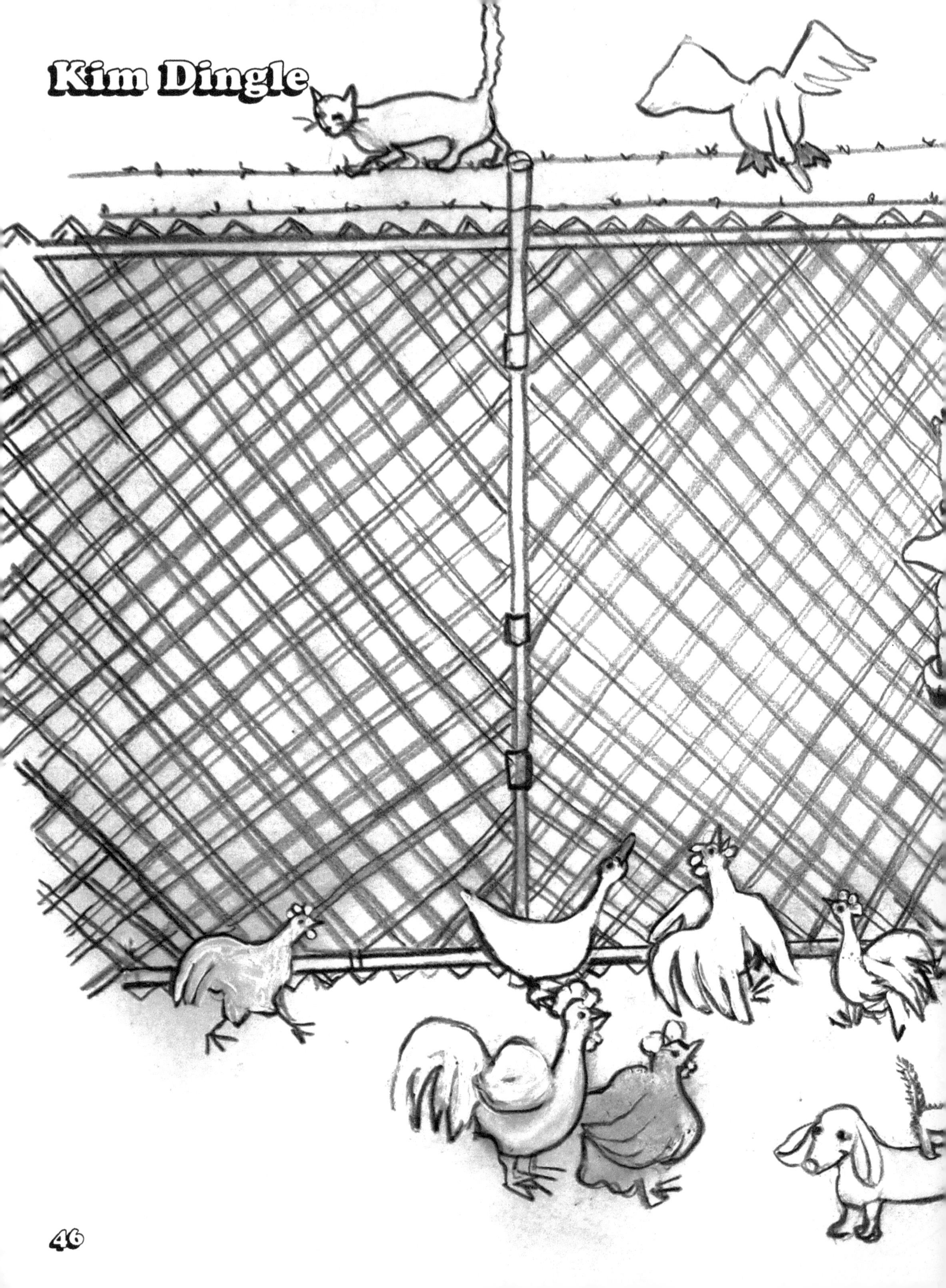

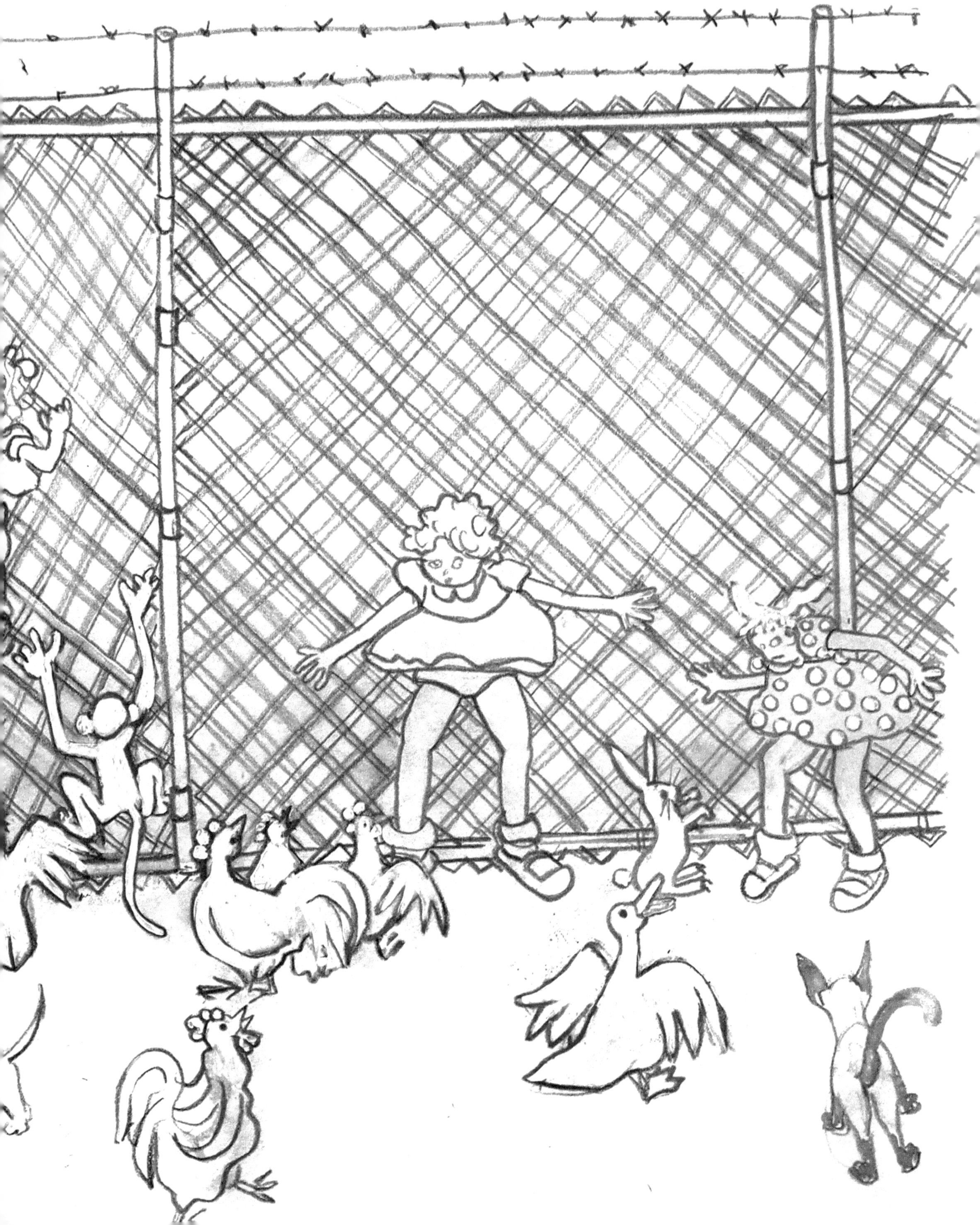

Mark Dion

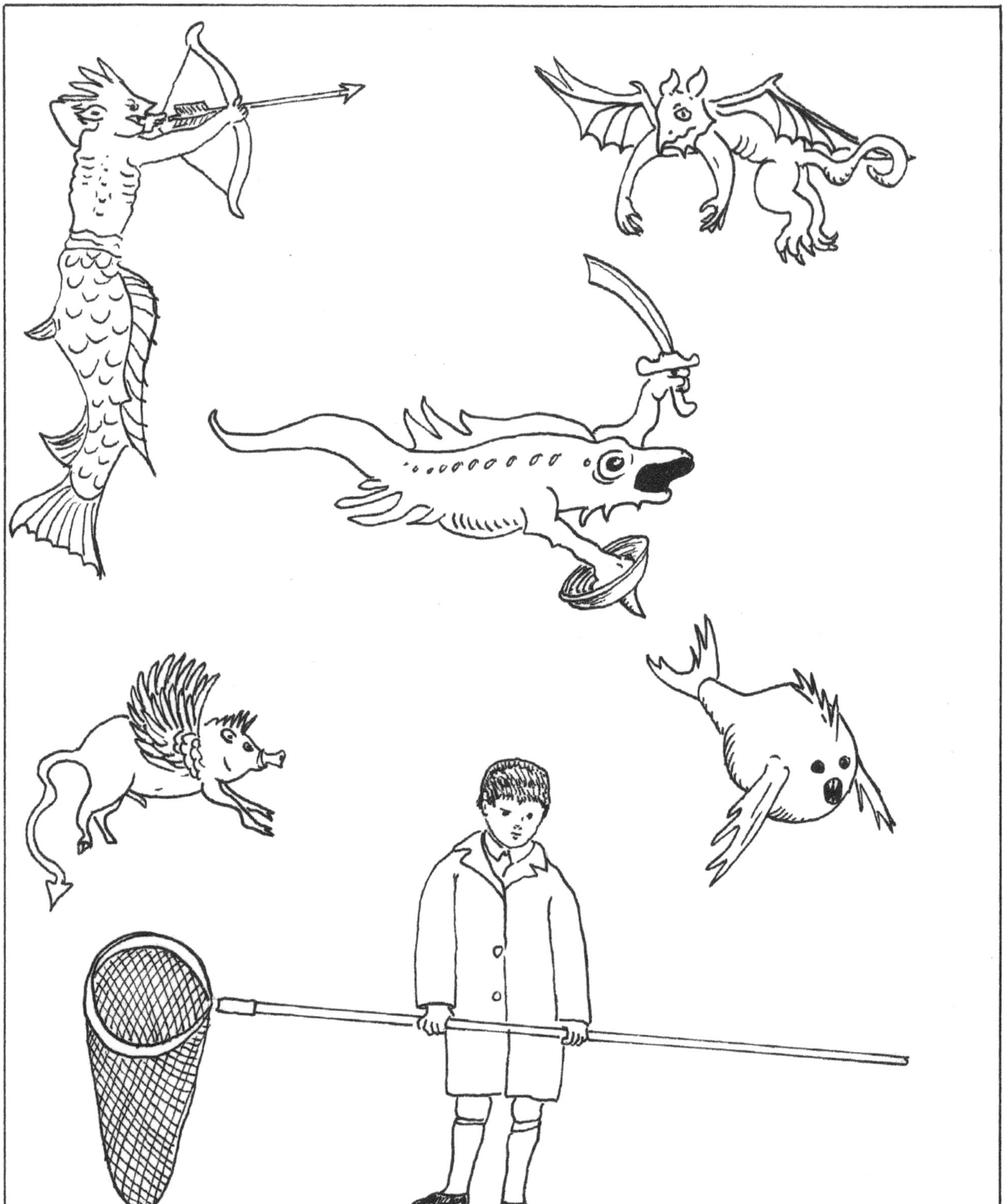

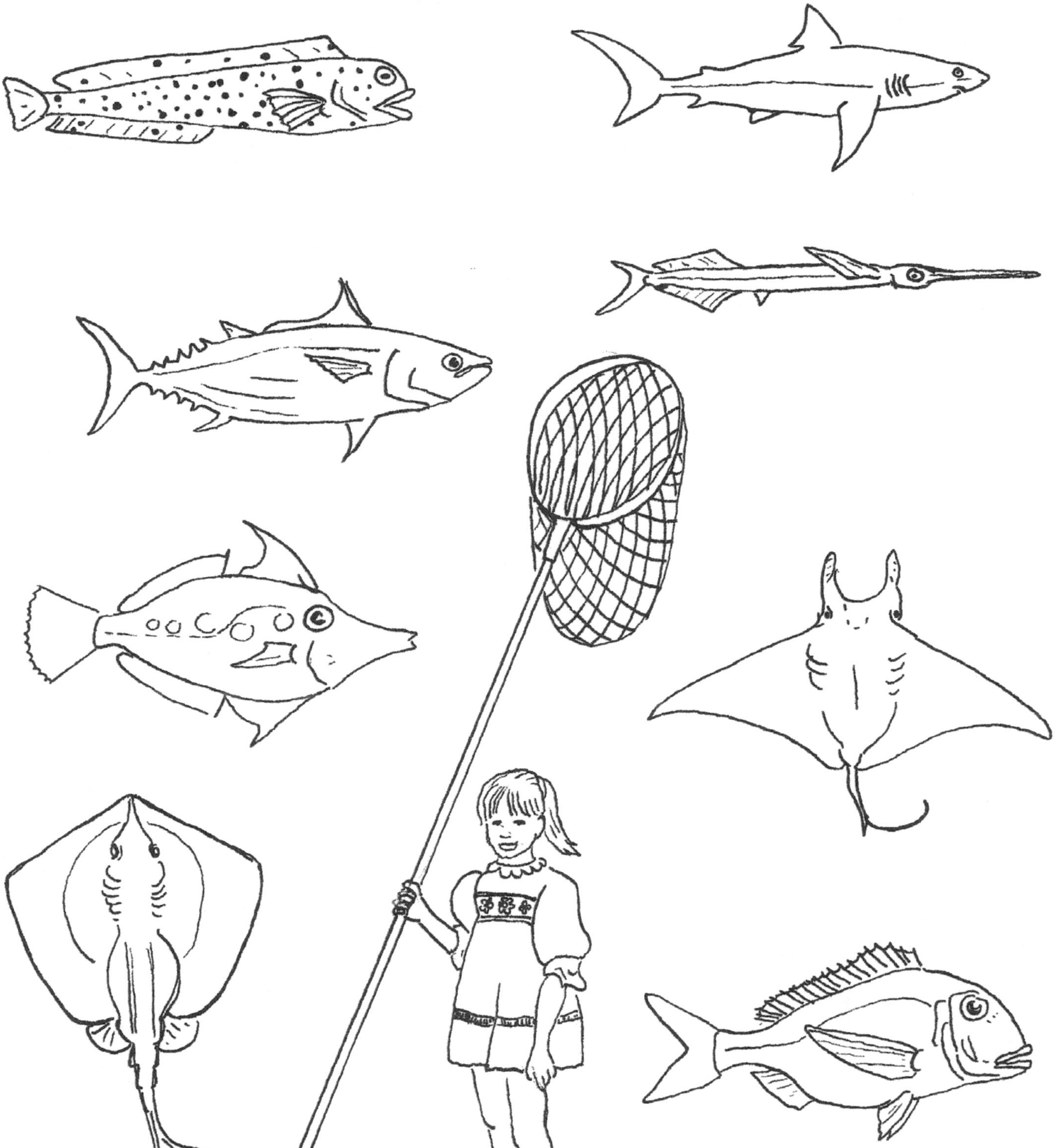

The Young Ichthyologist   M. Dion 2015

Evan Gruzis

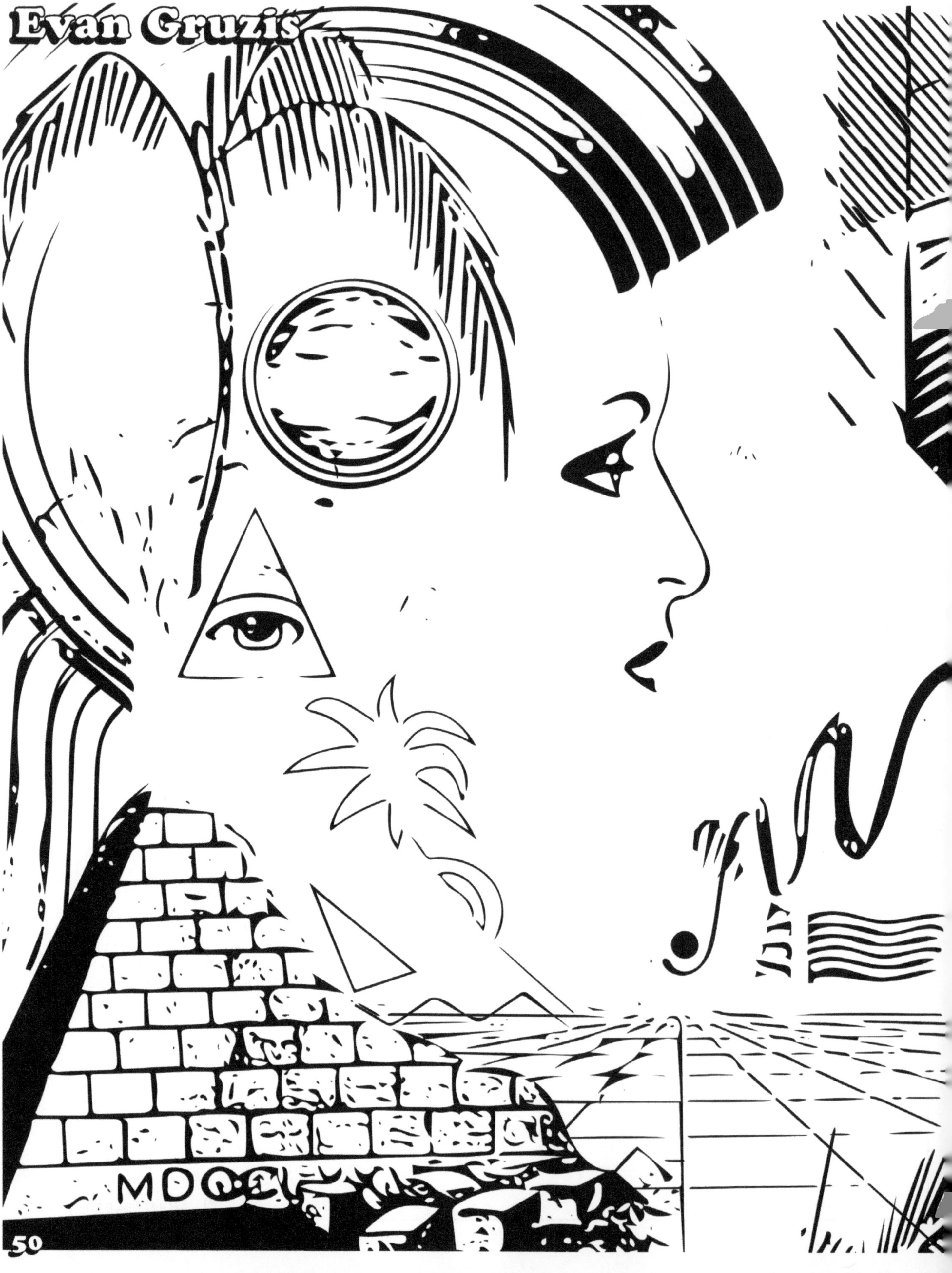

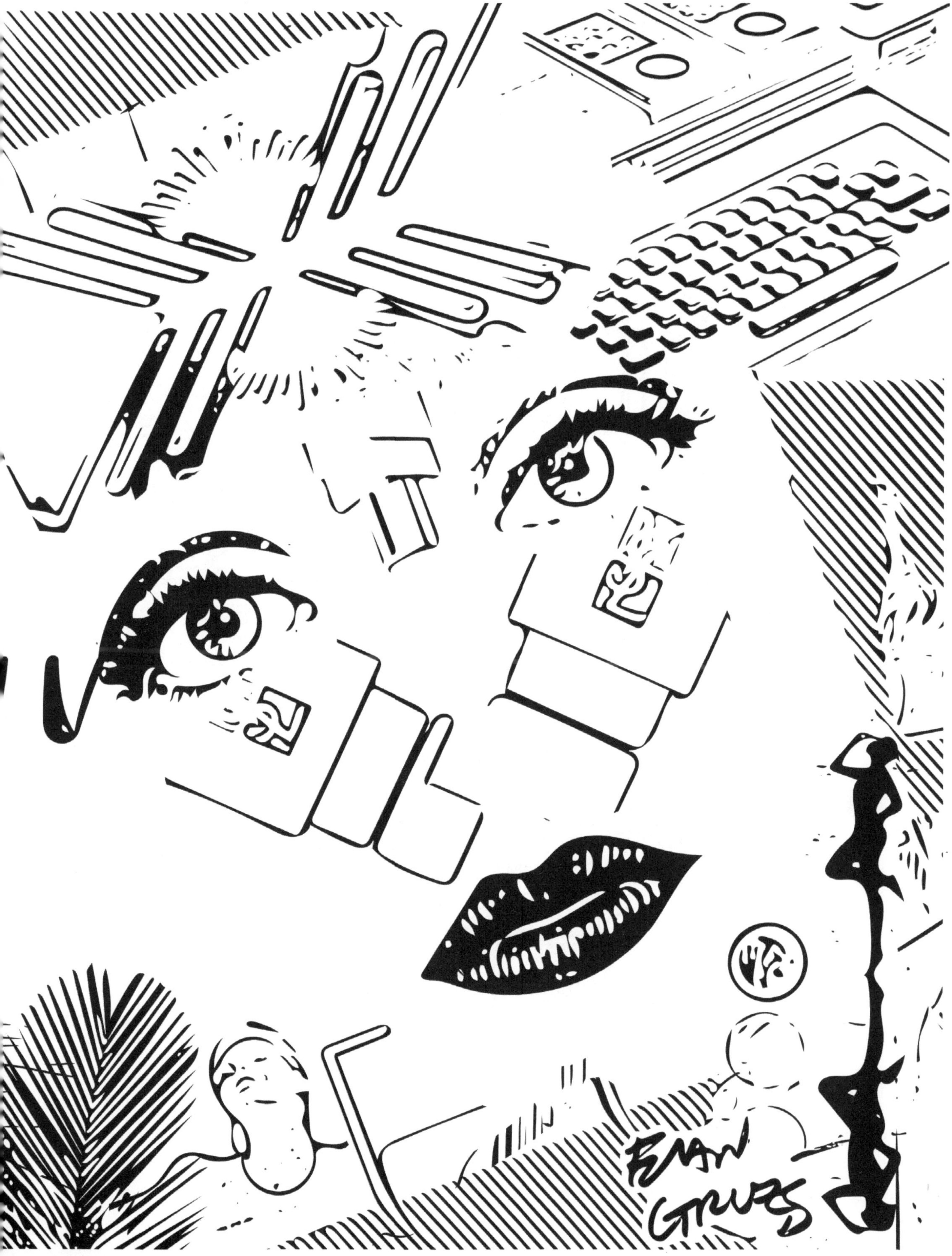

Subodh Gupta

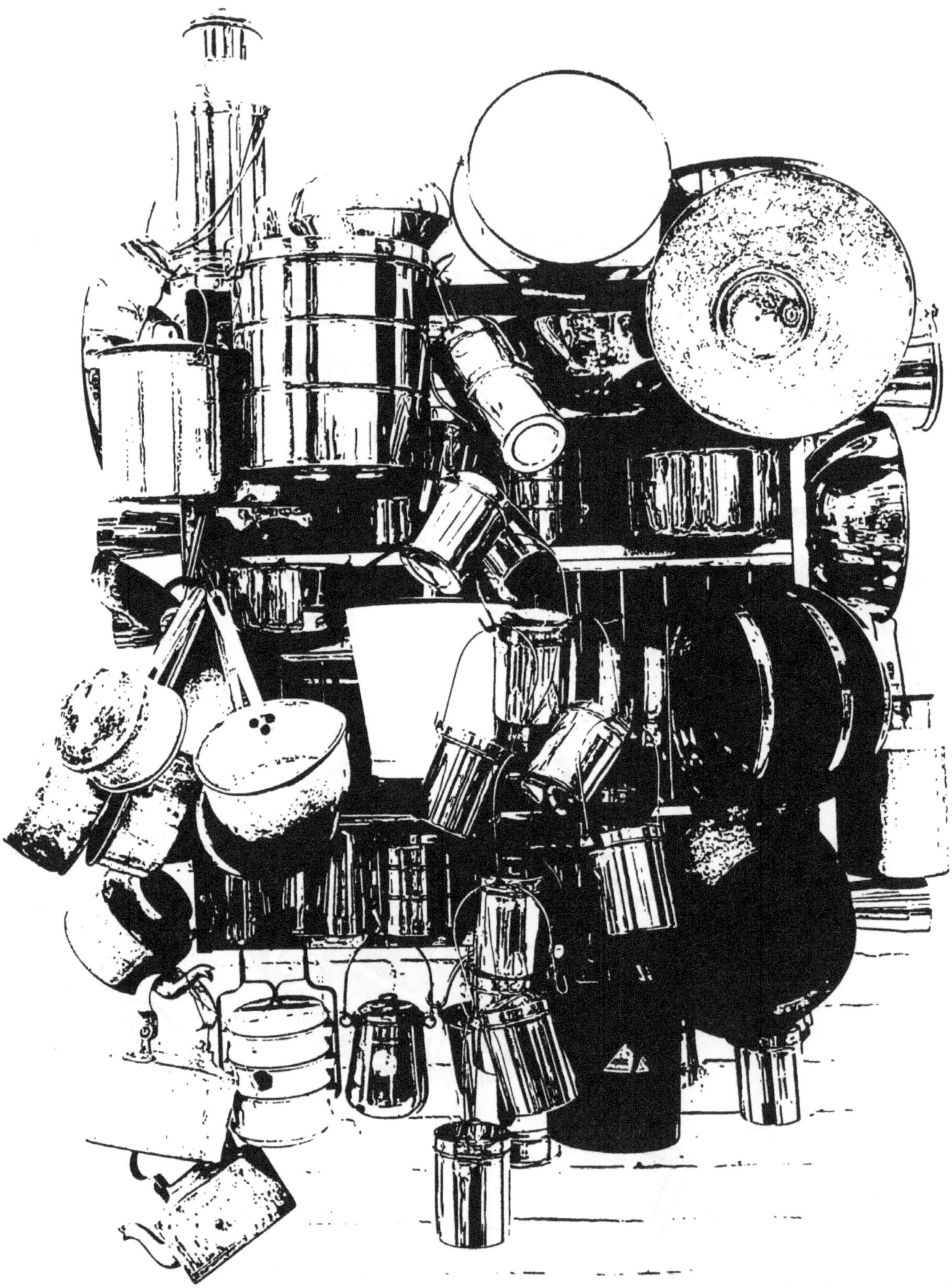

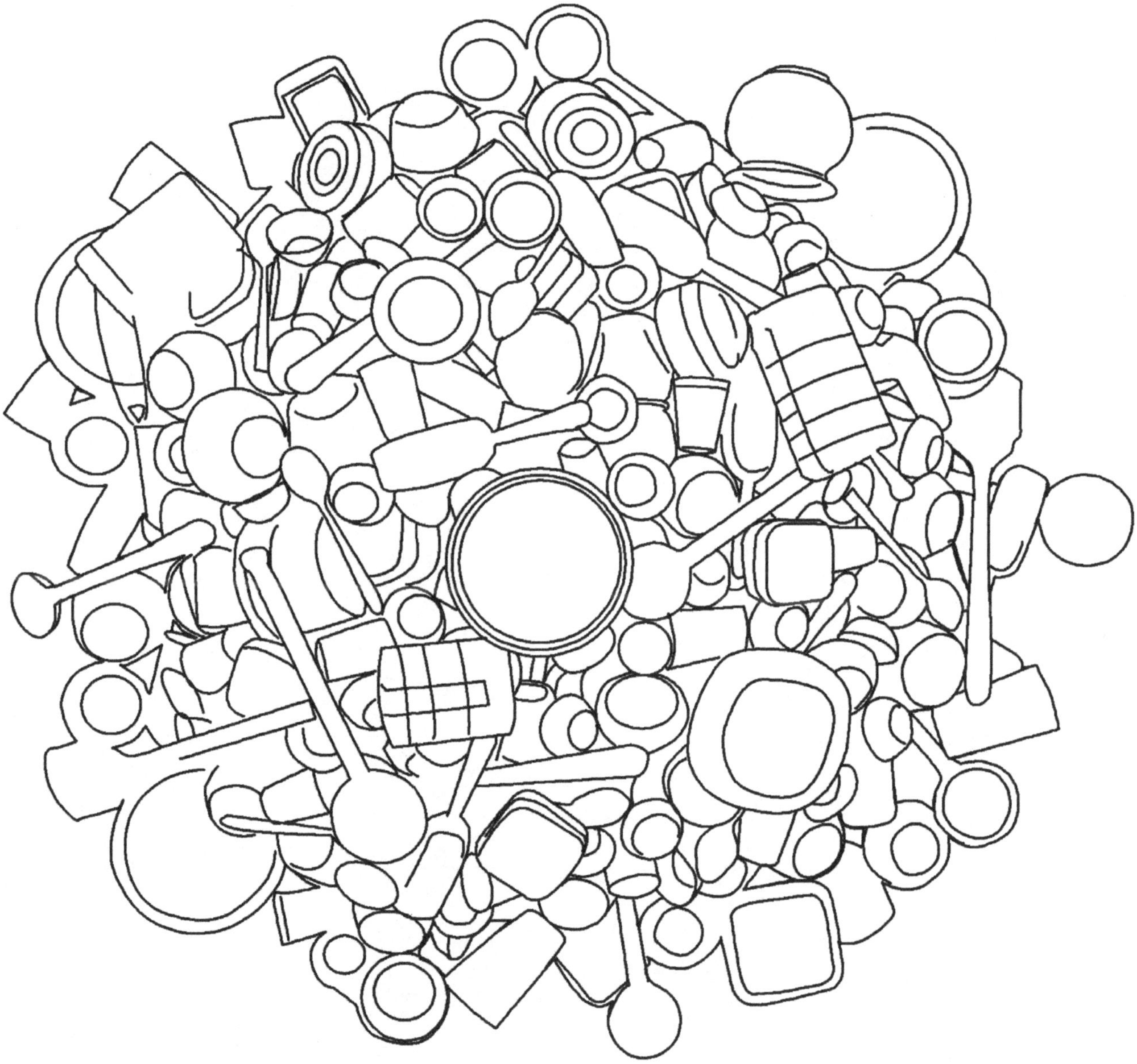

Mark Hagen

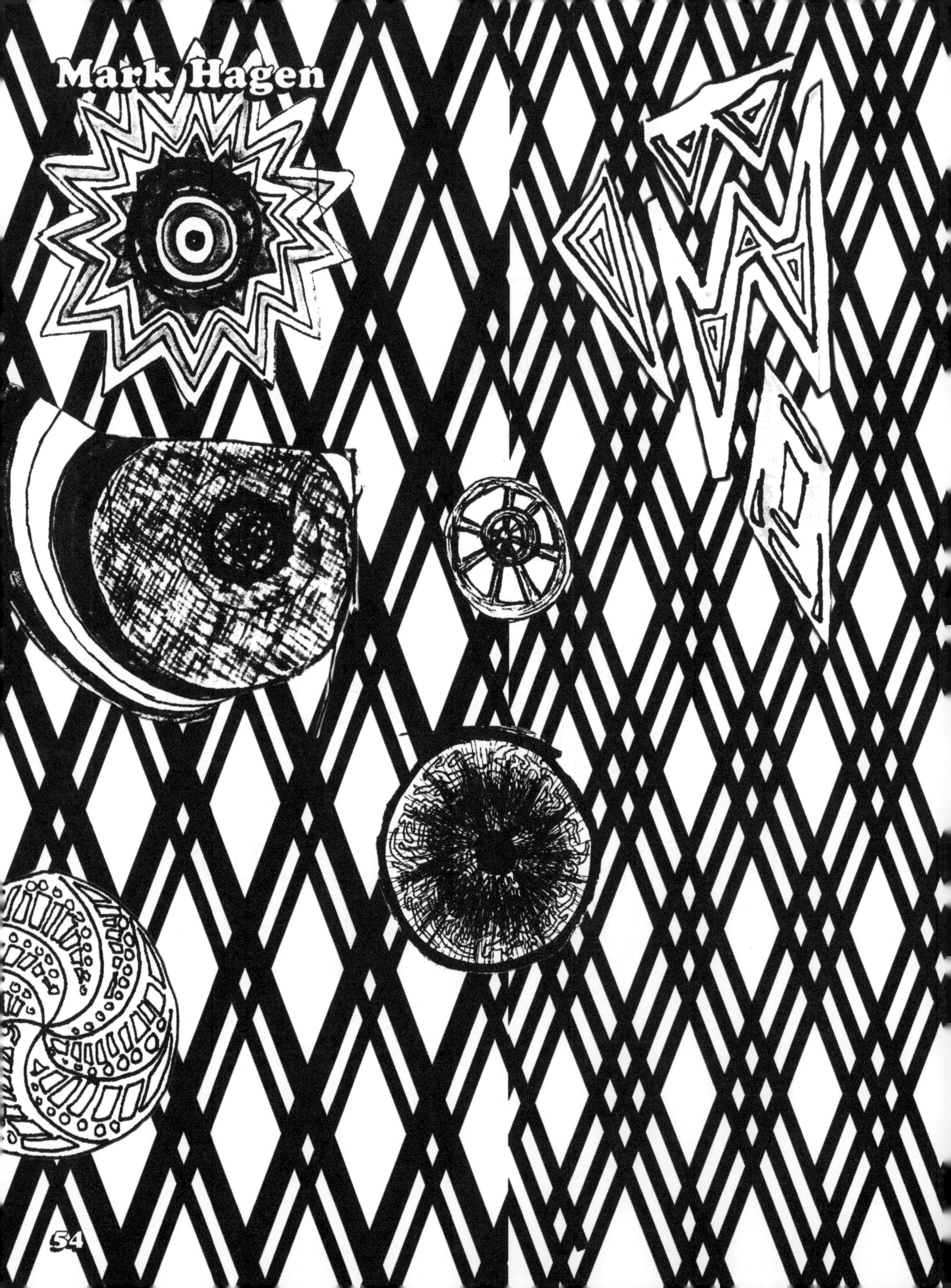

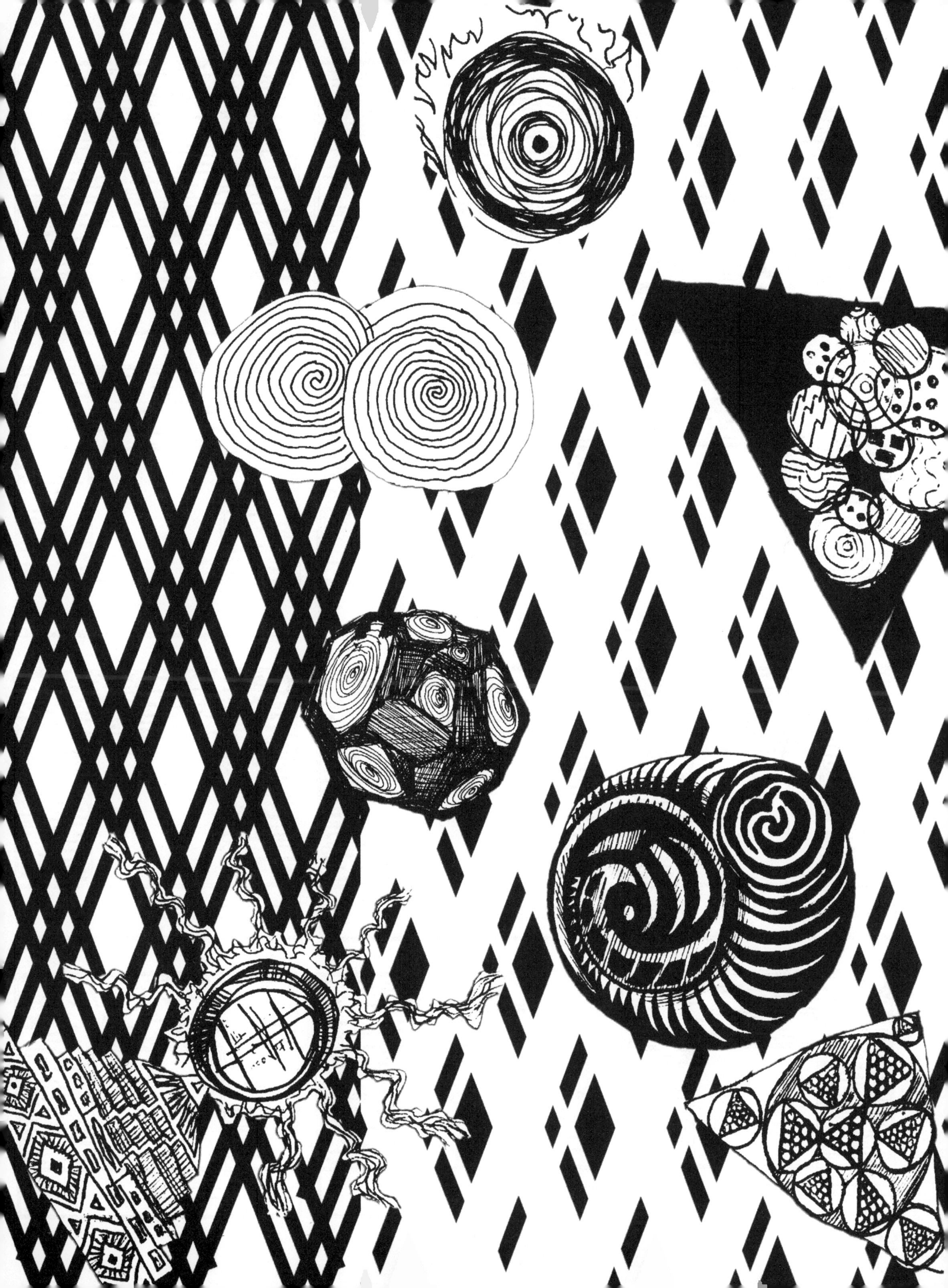

Peter Halley

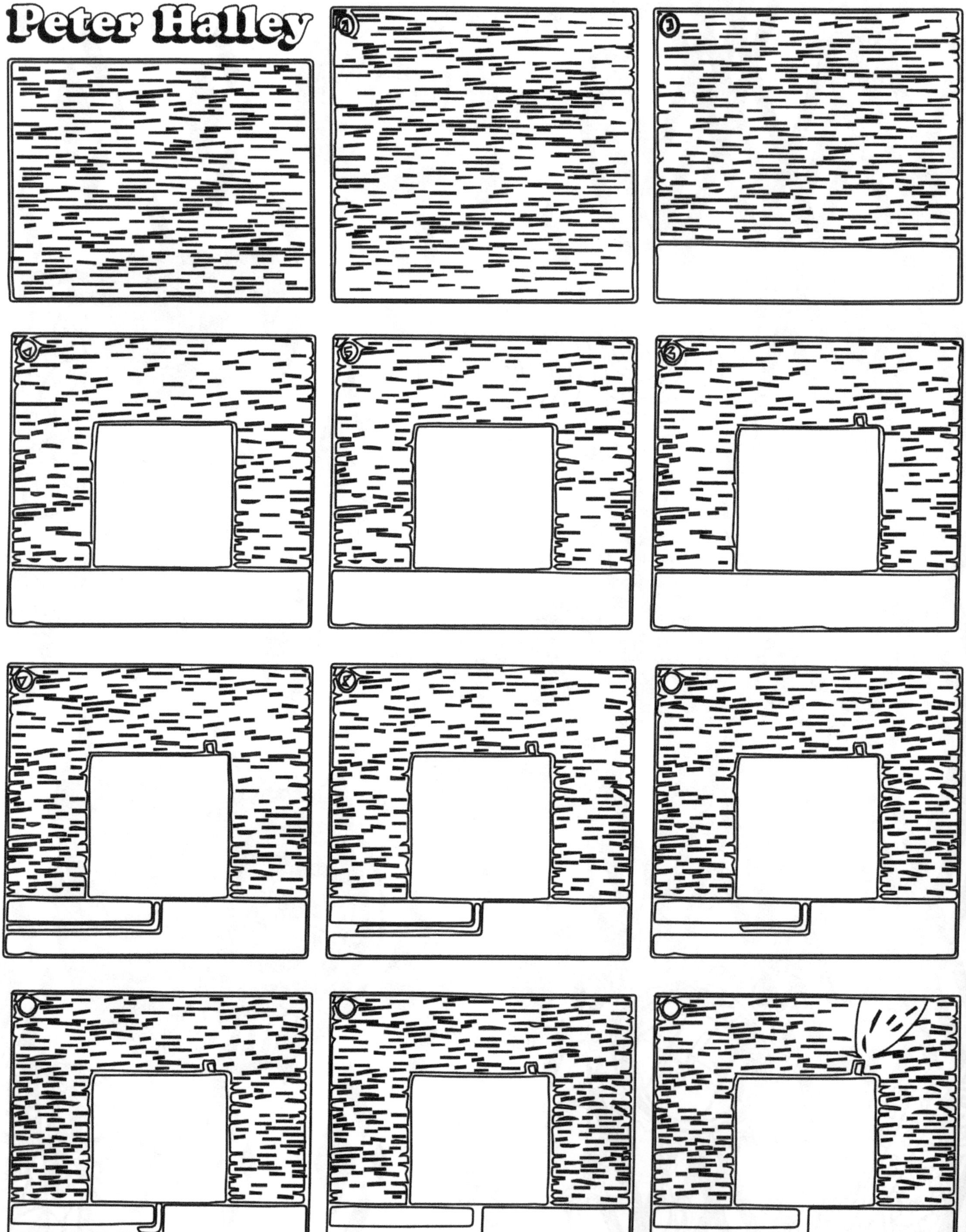

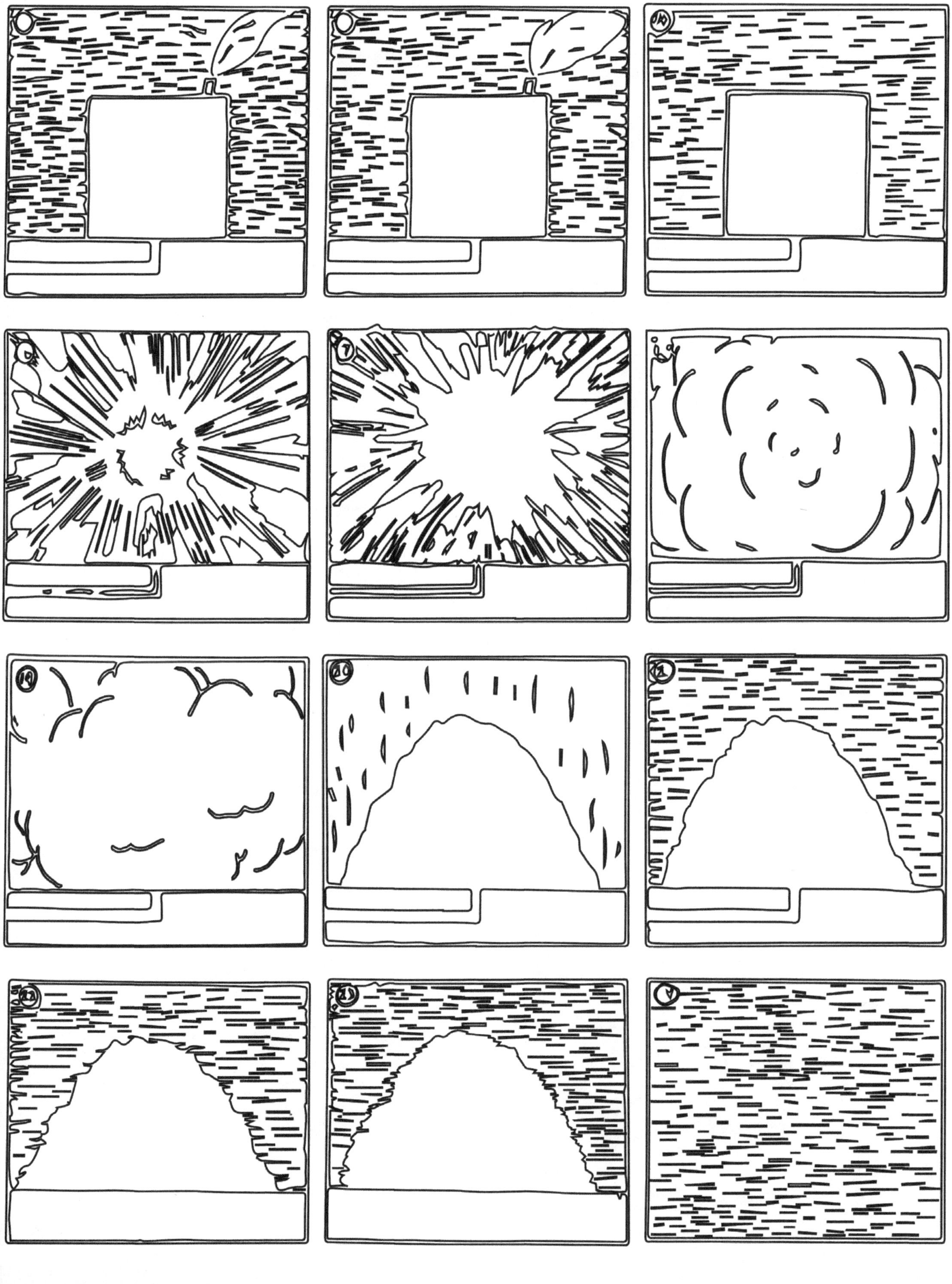

Keith Haring

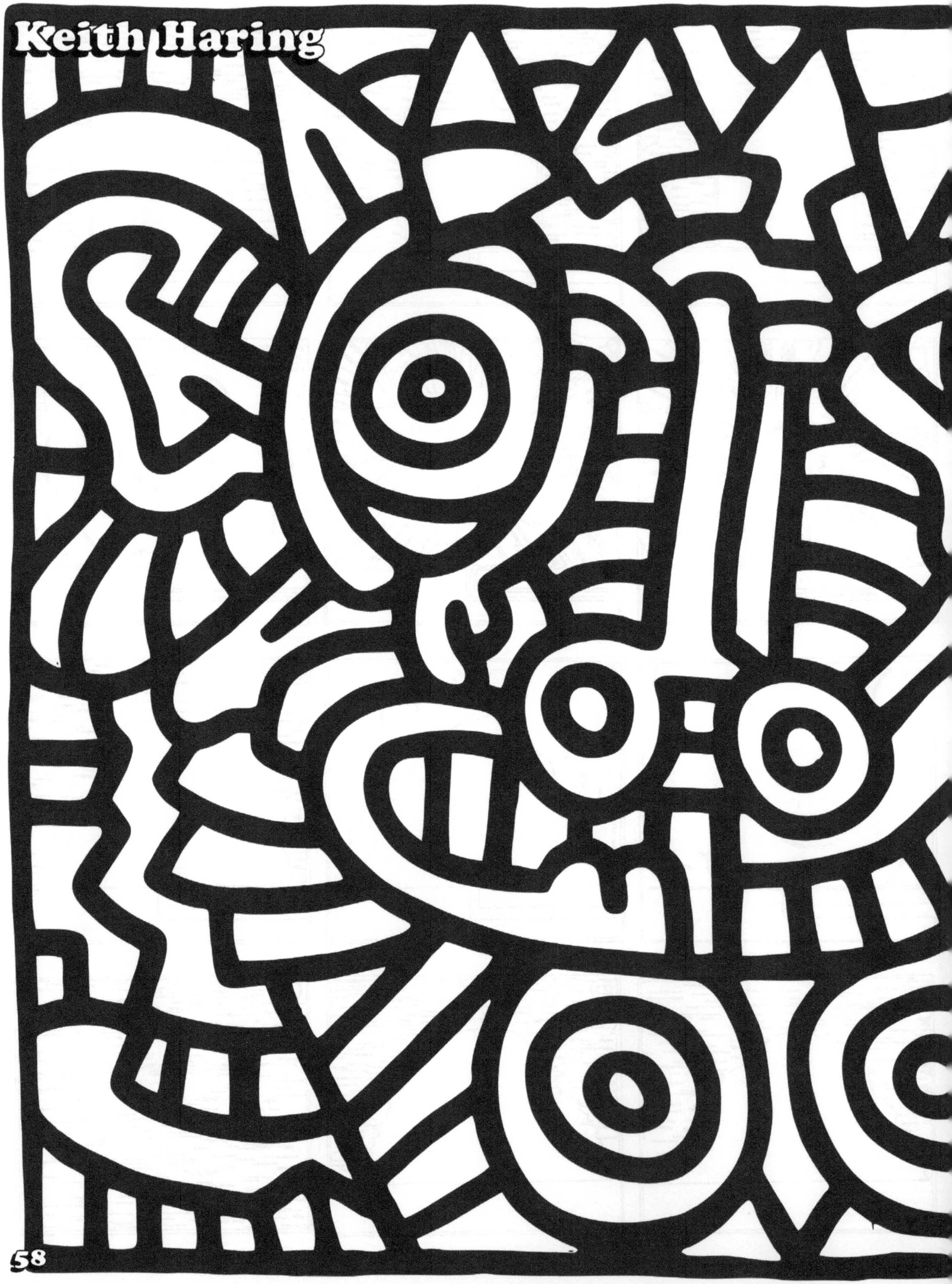

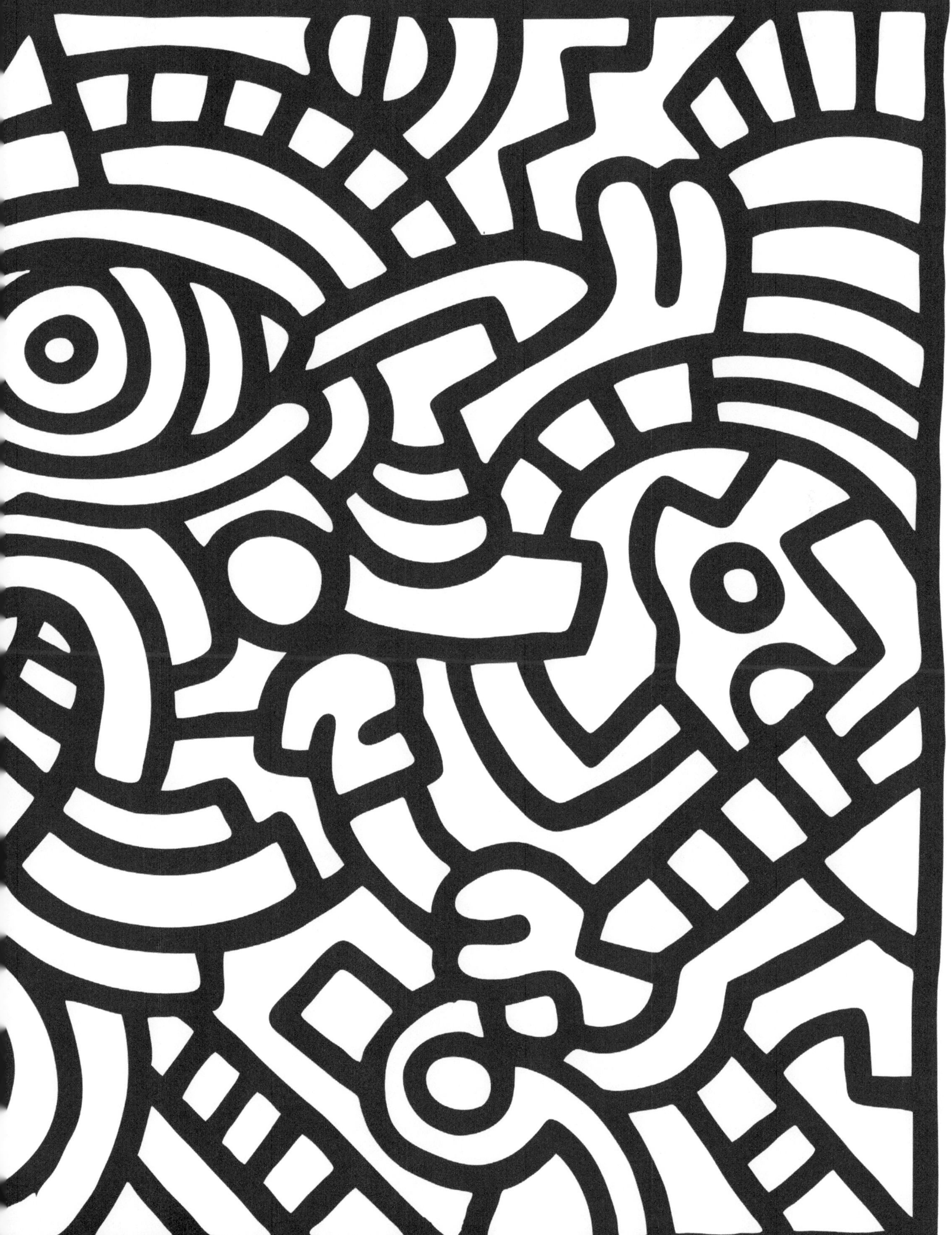

Alex Israel

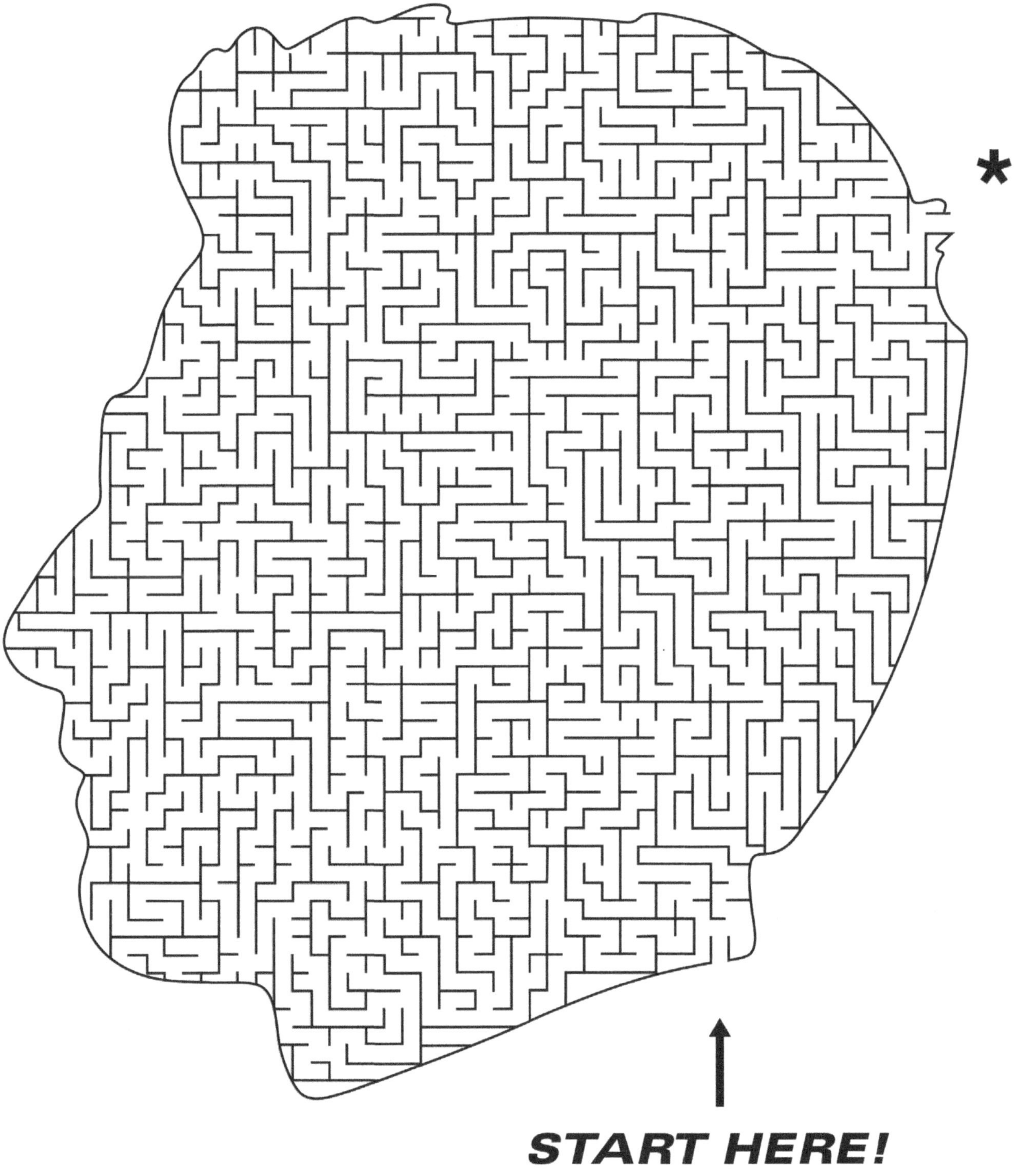

START HERE!

Rashid Johnson

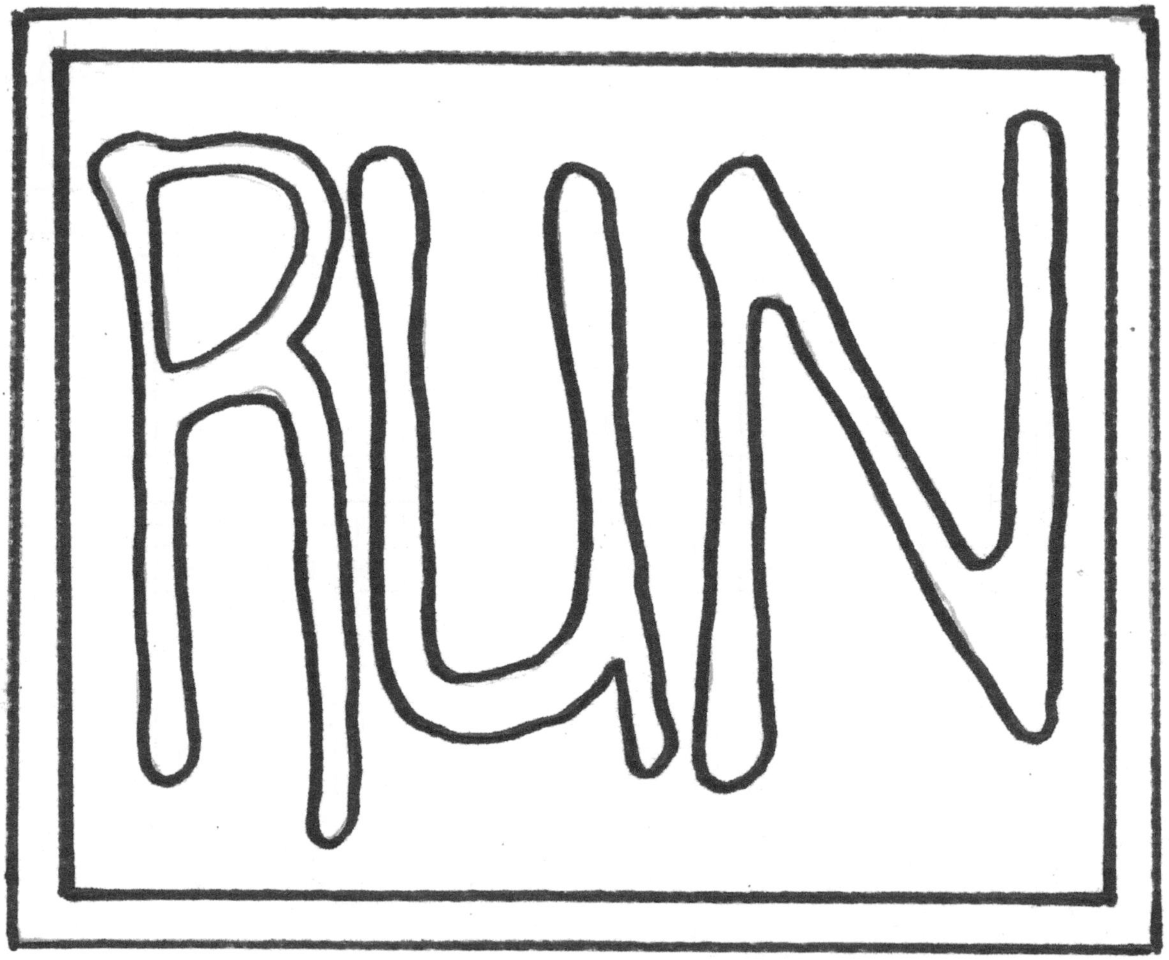

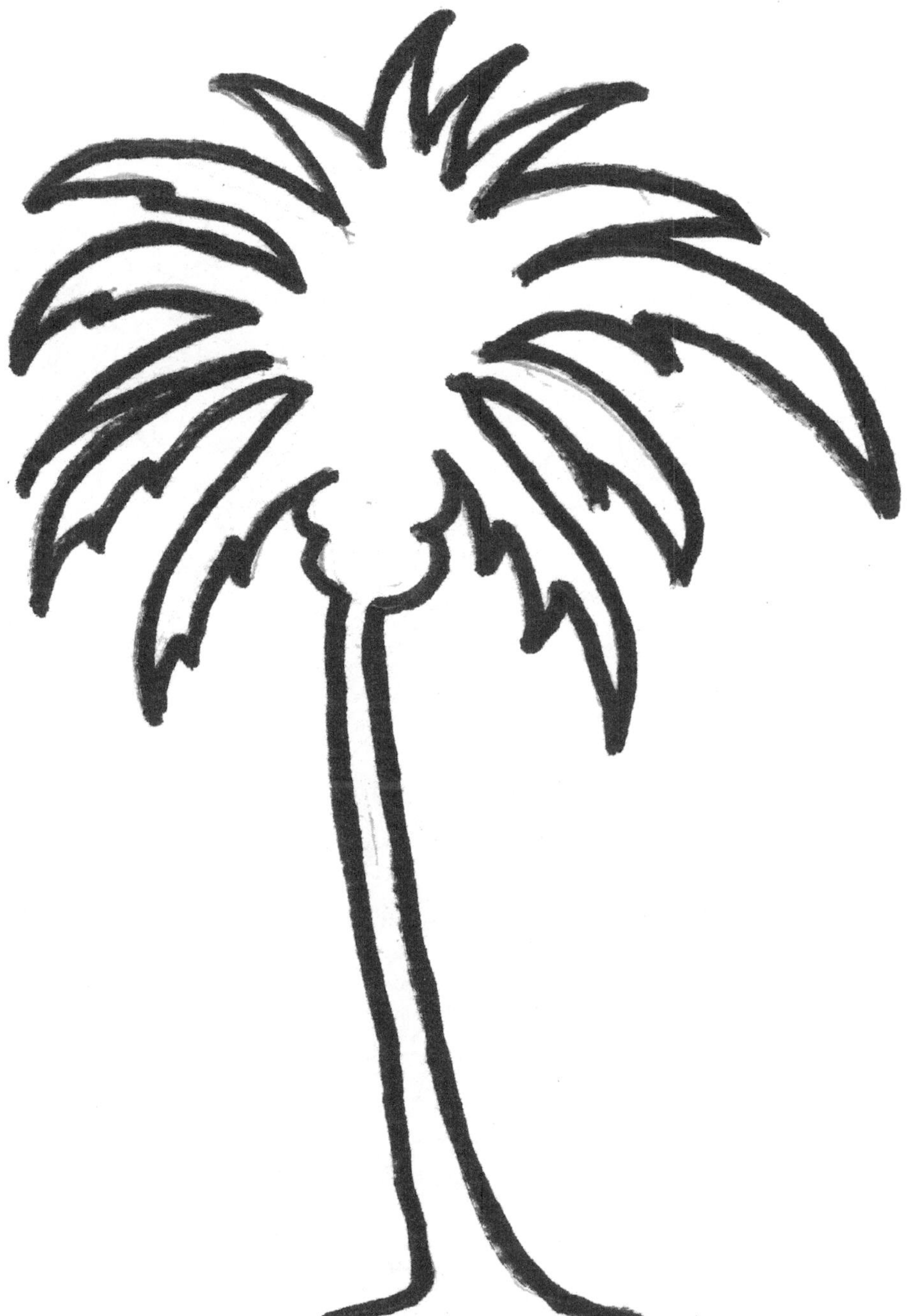

Glenn Kaino

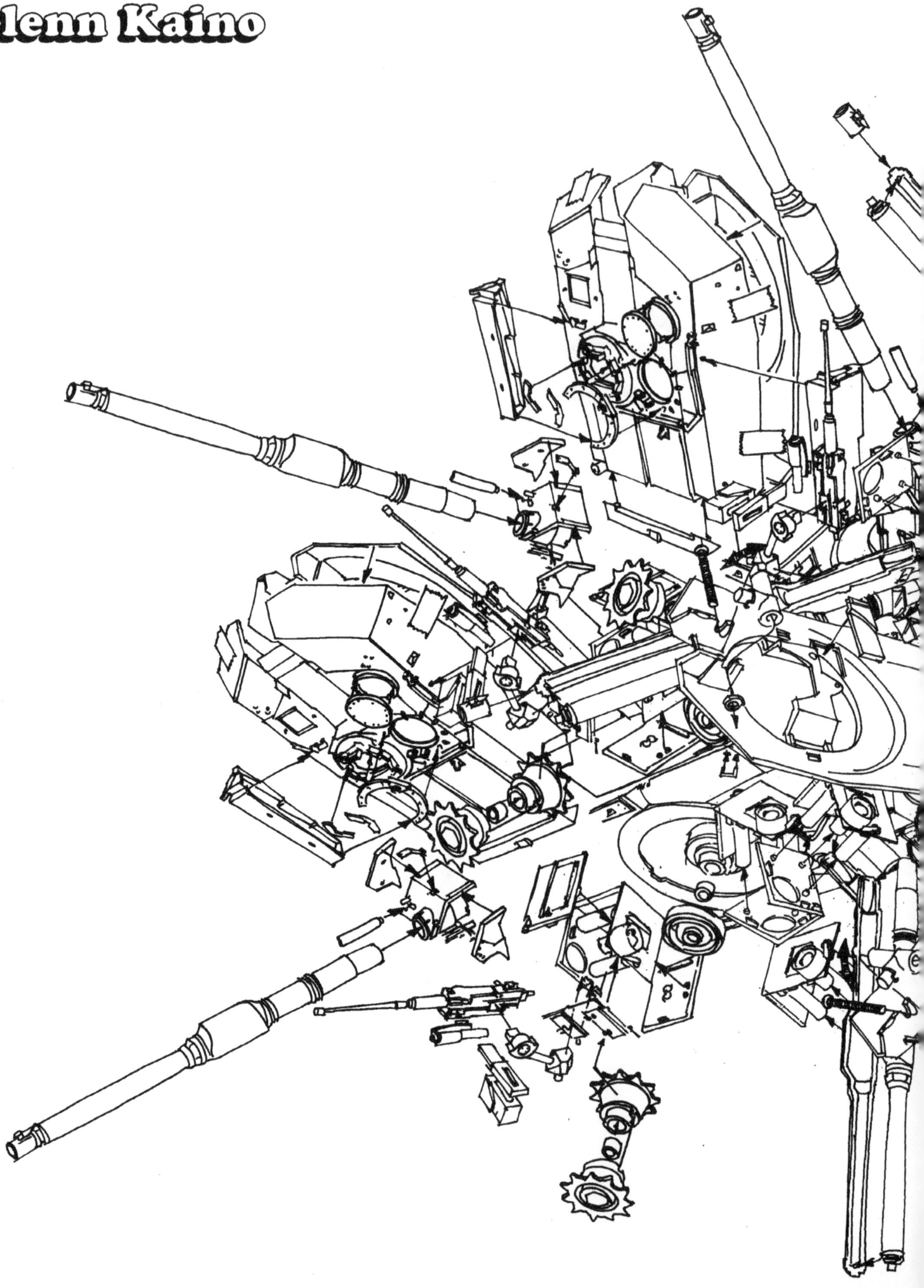

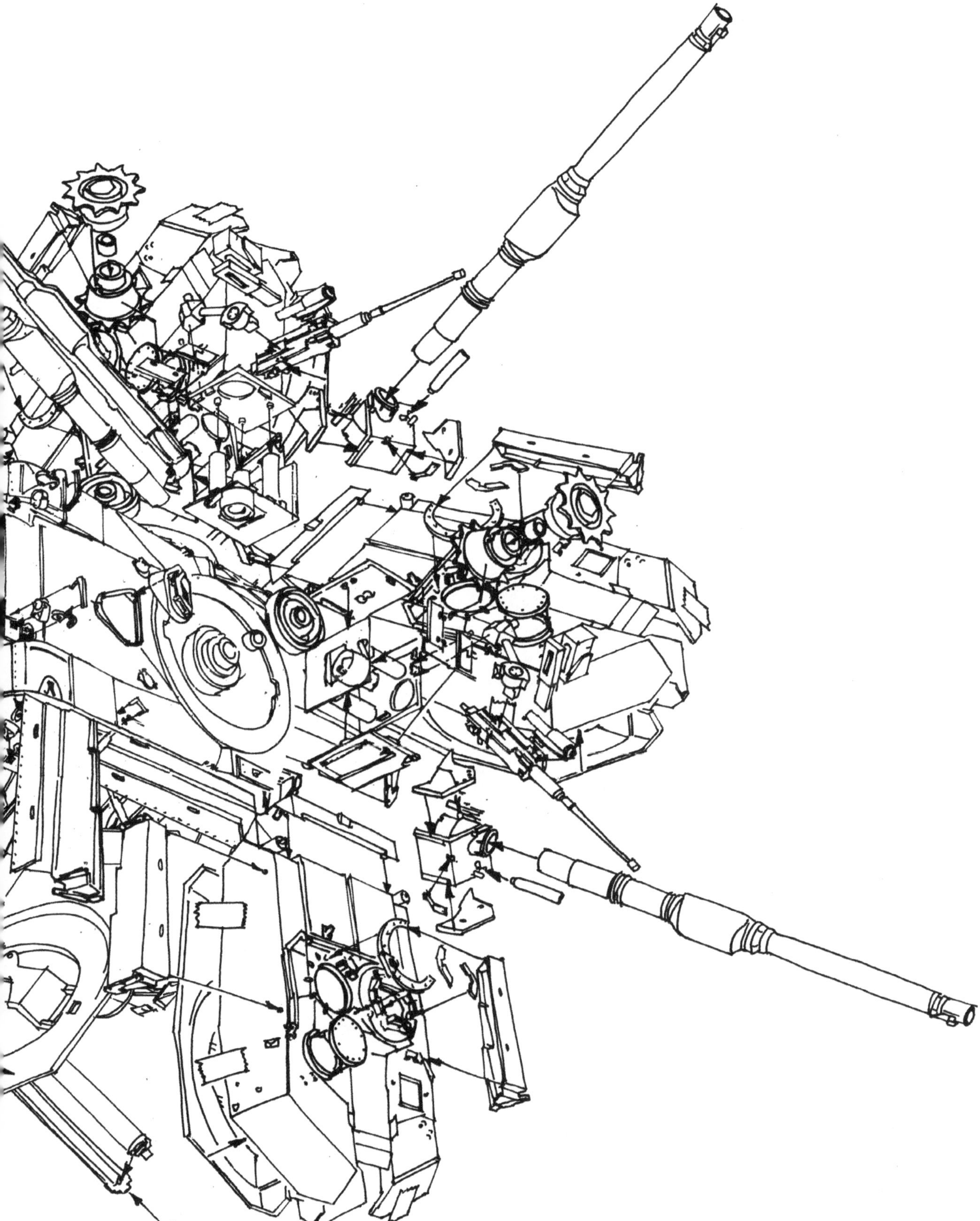

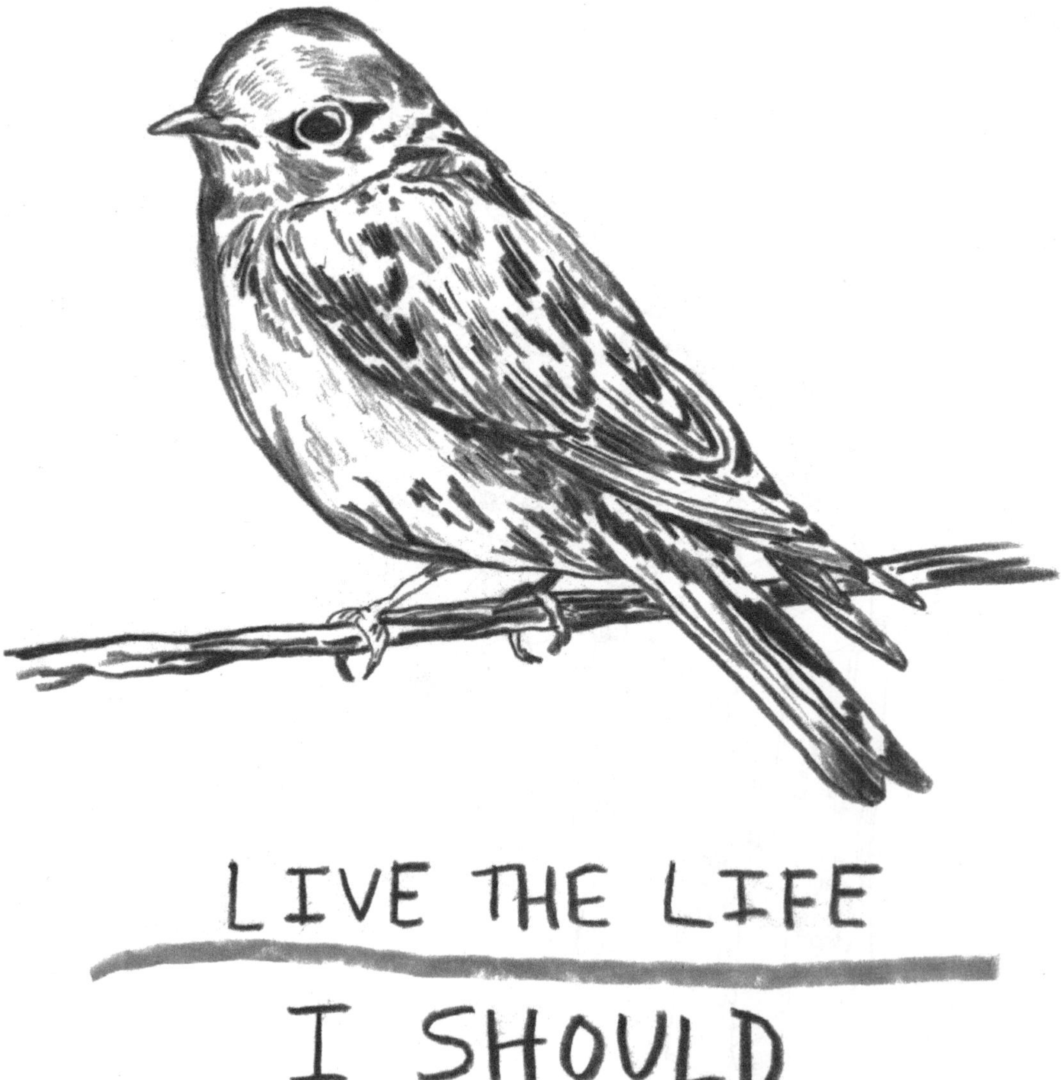
LIVE THE LIFE
I SHOULD

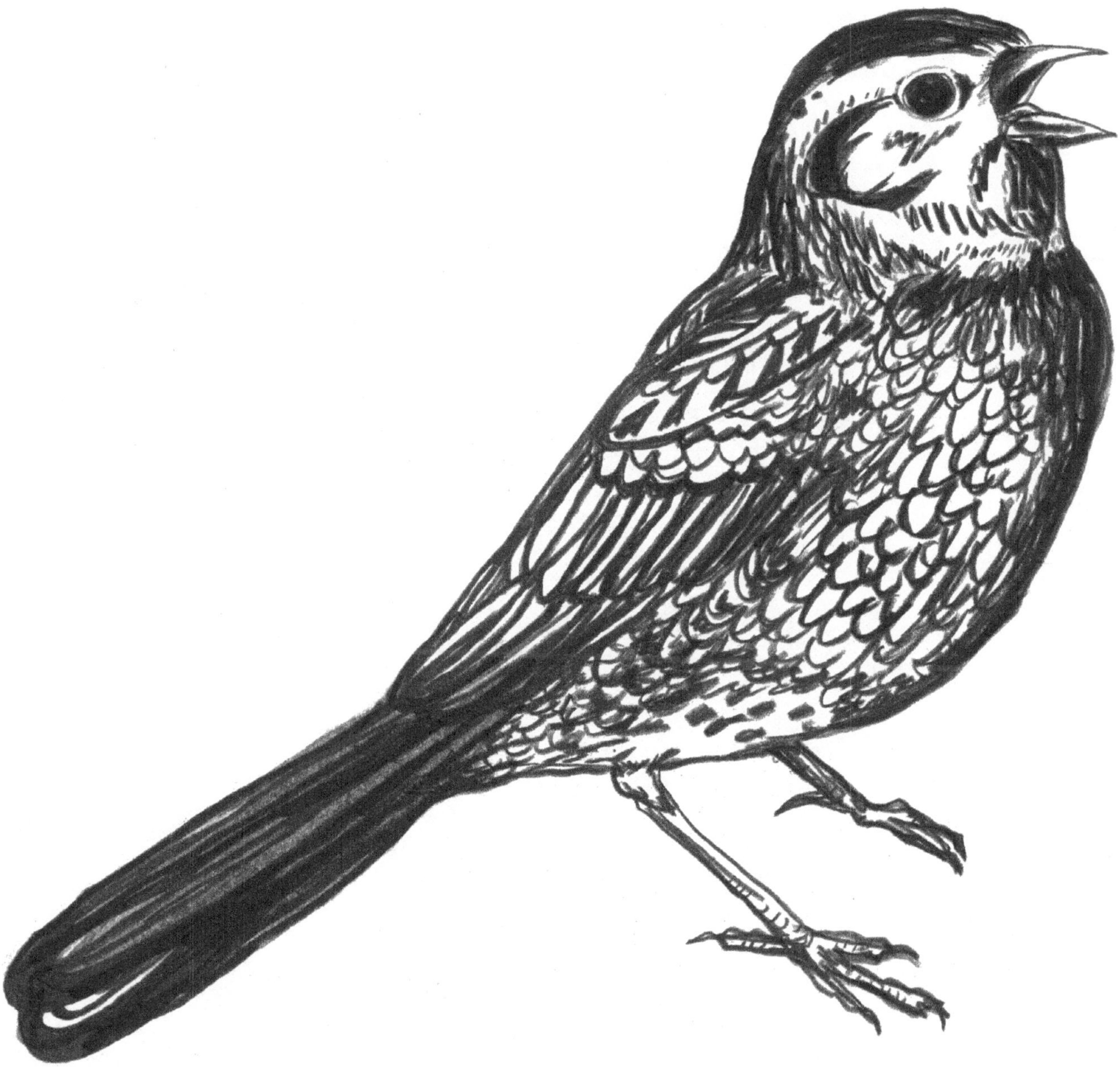

RENEWAL

RENEWAL

Greg Lindquist

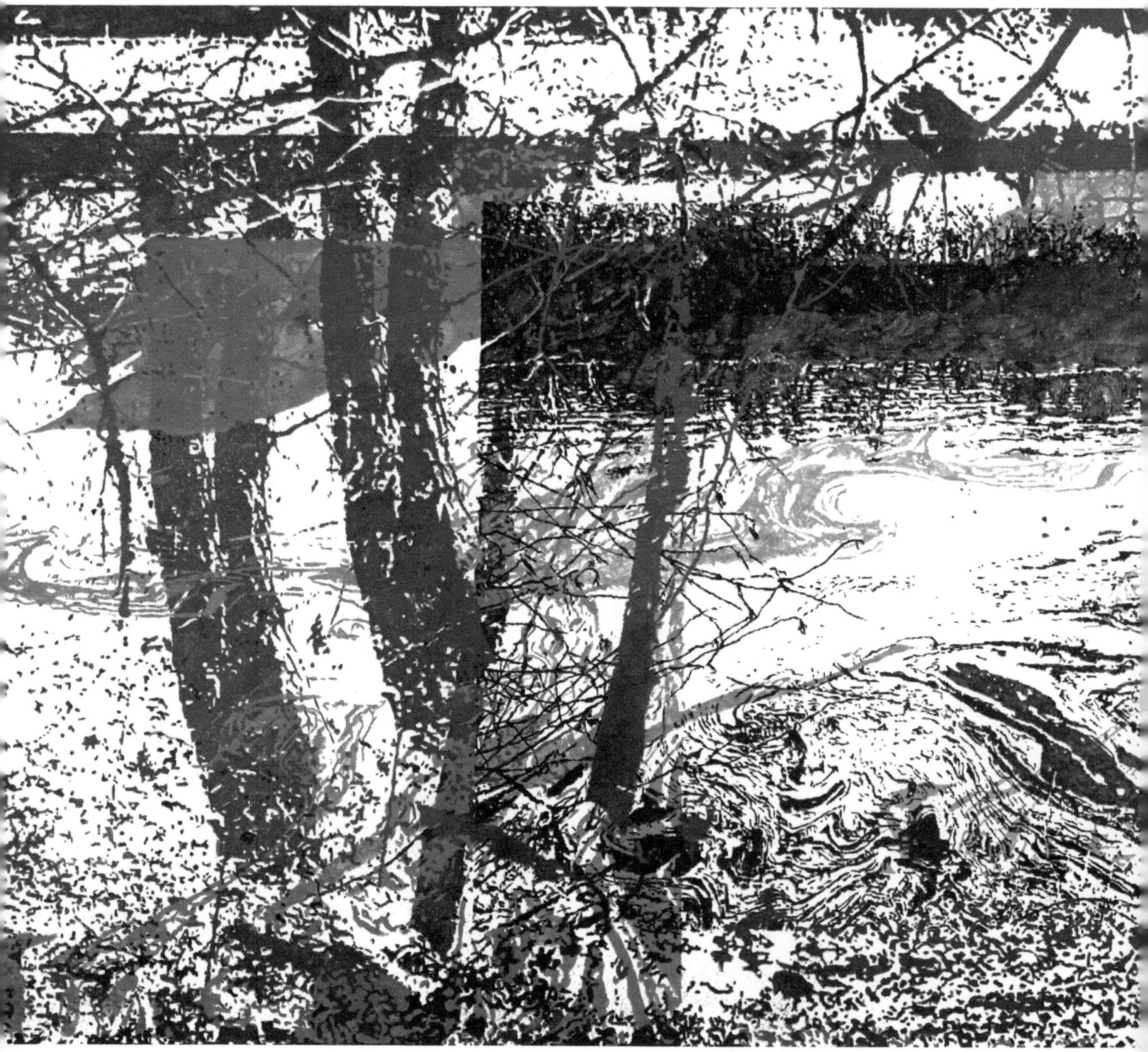

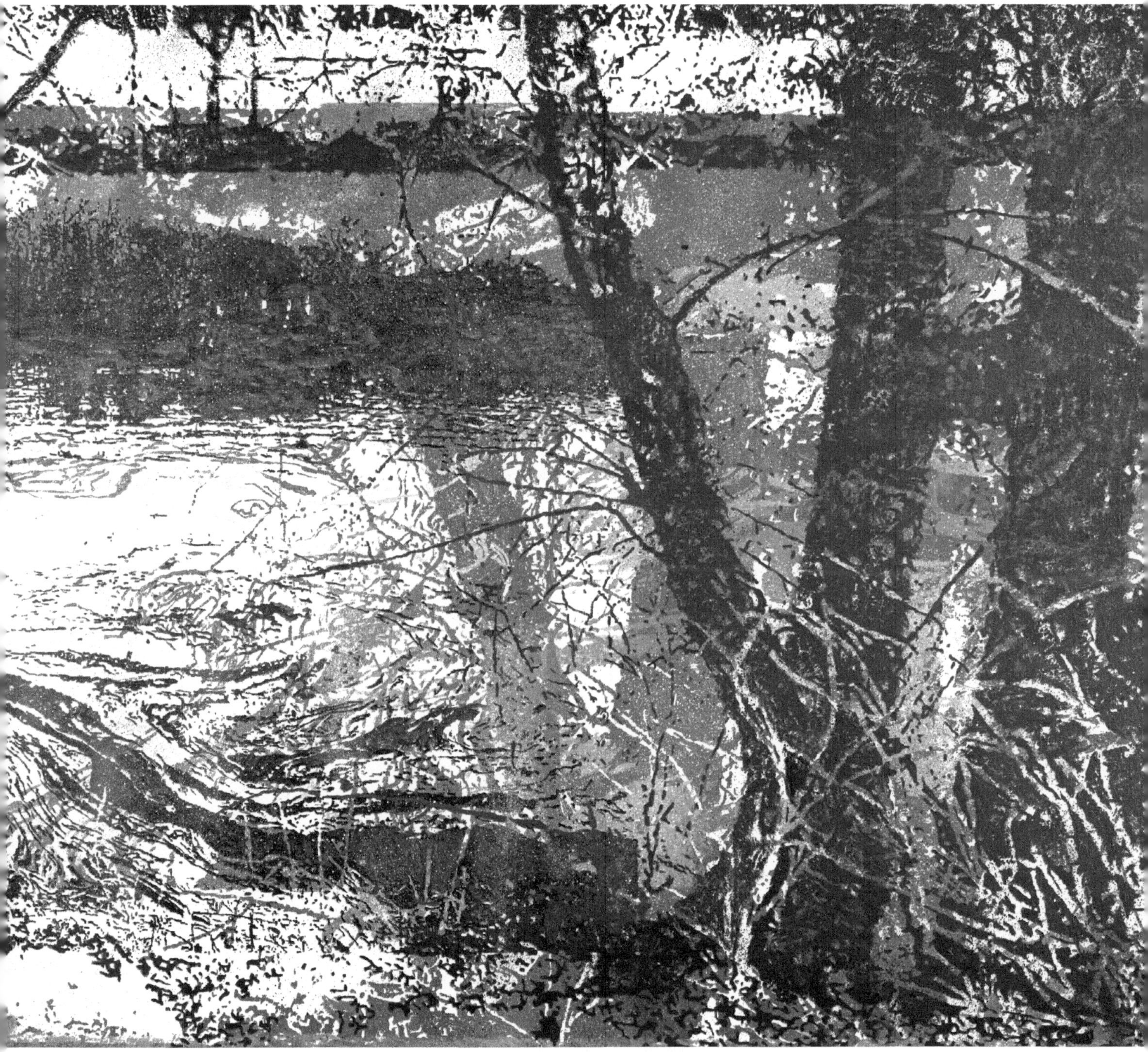

Liu Ye

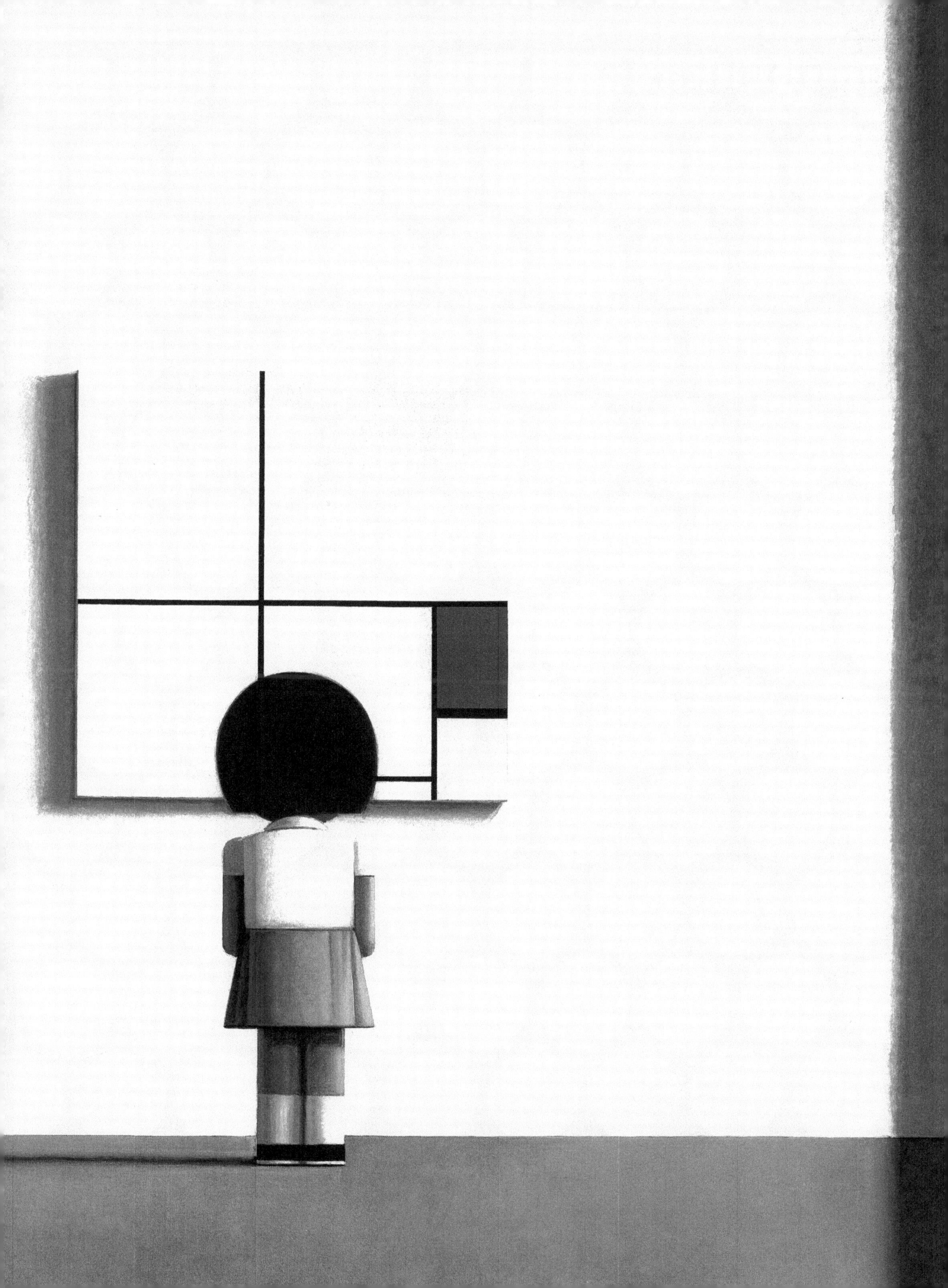

Emil Lukas

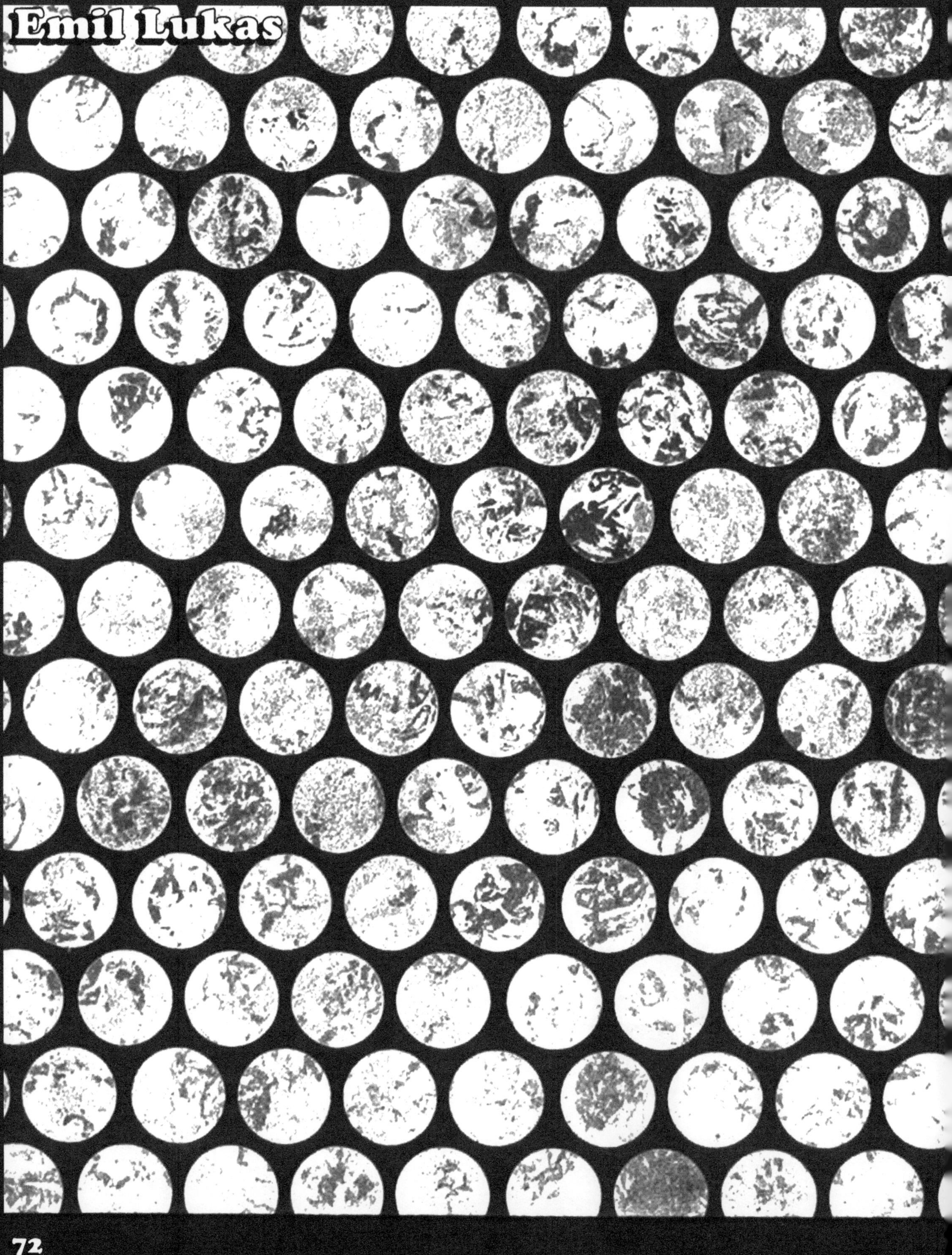

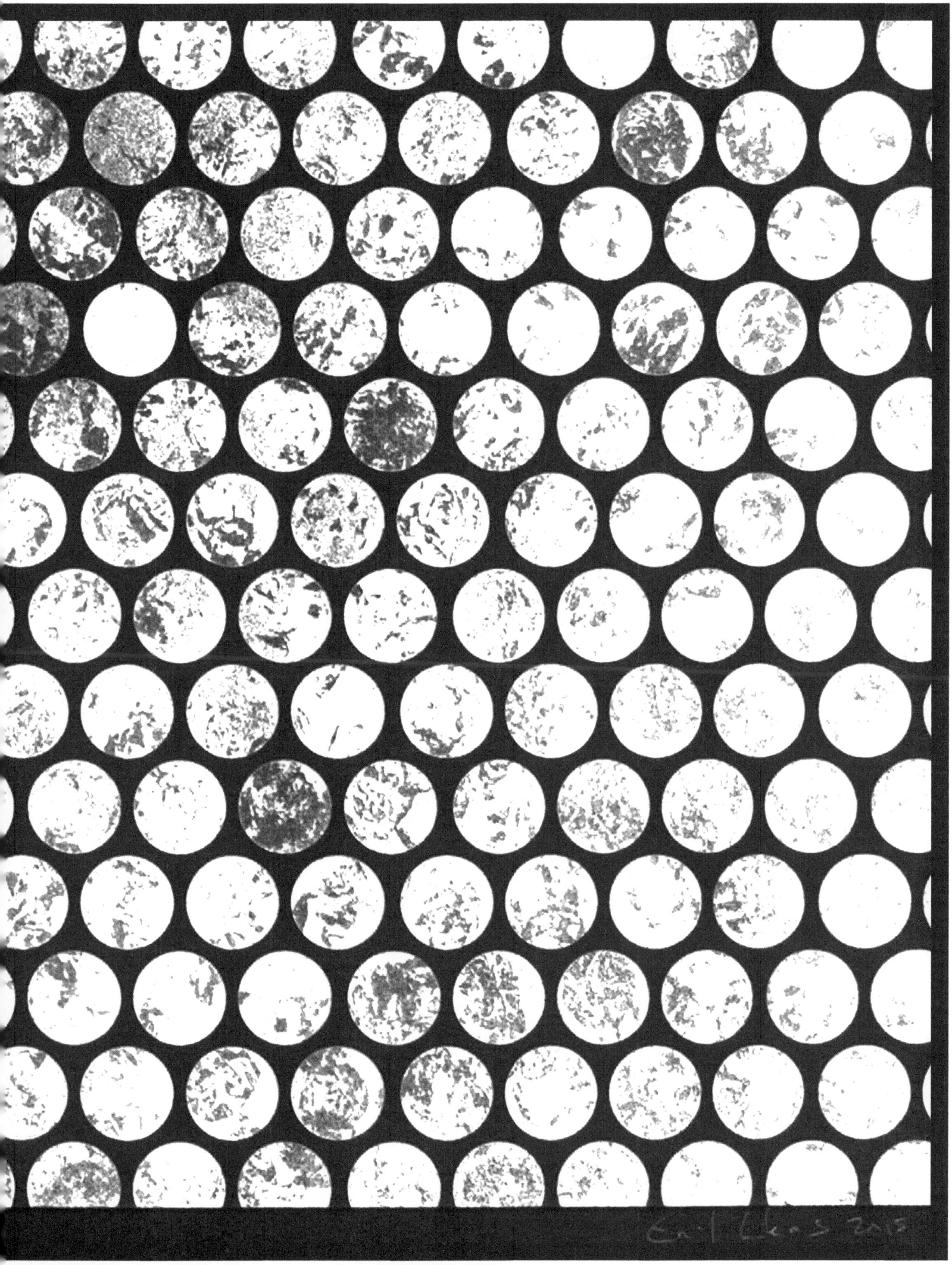

Ed McGowin

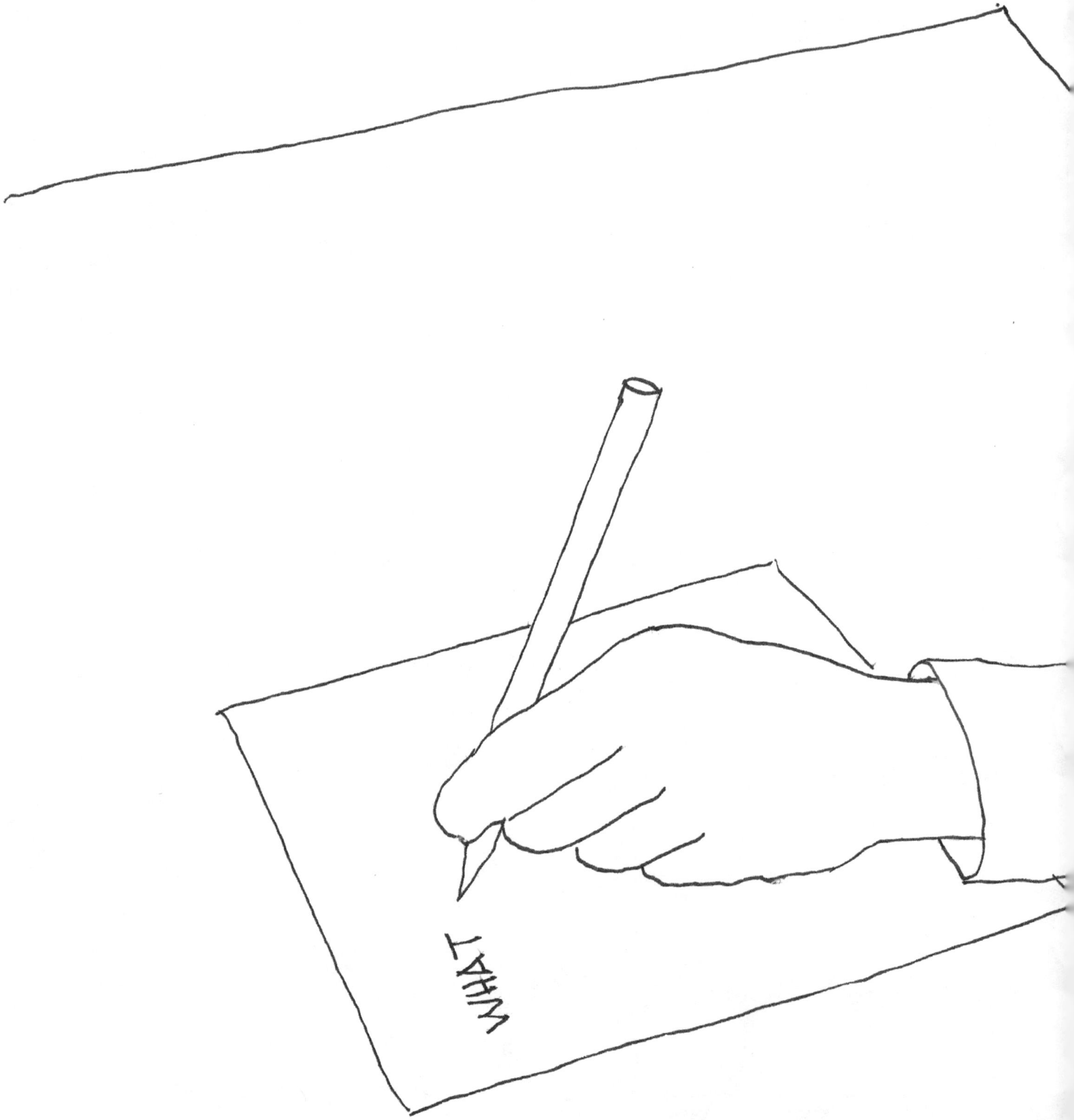

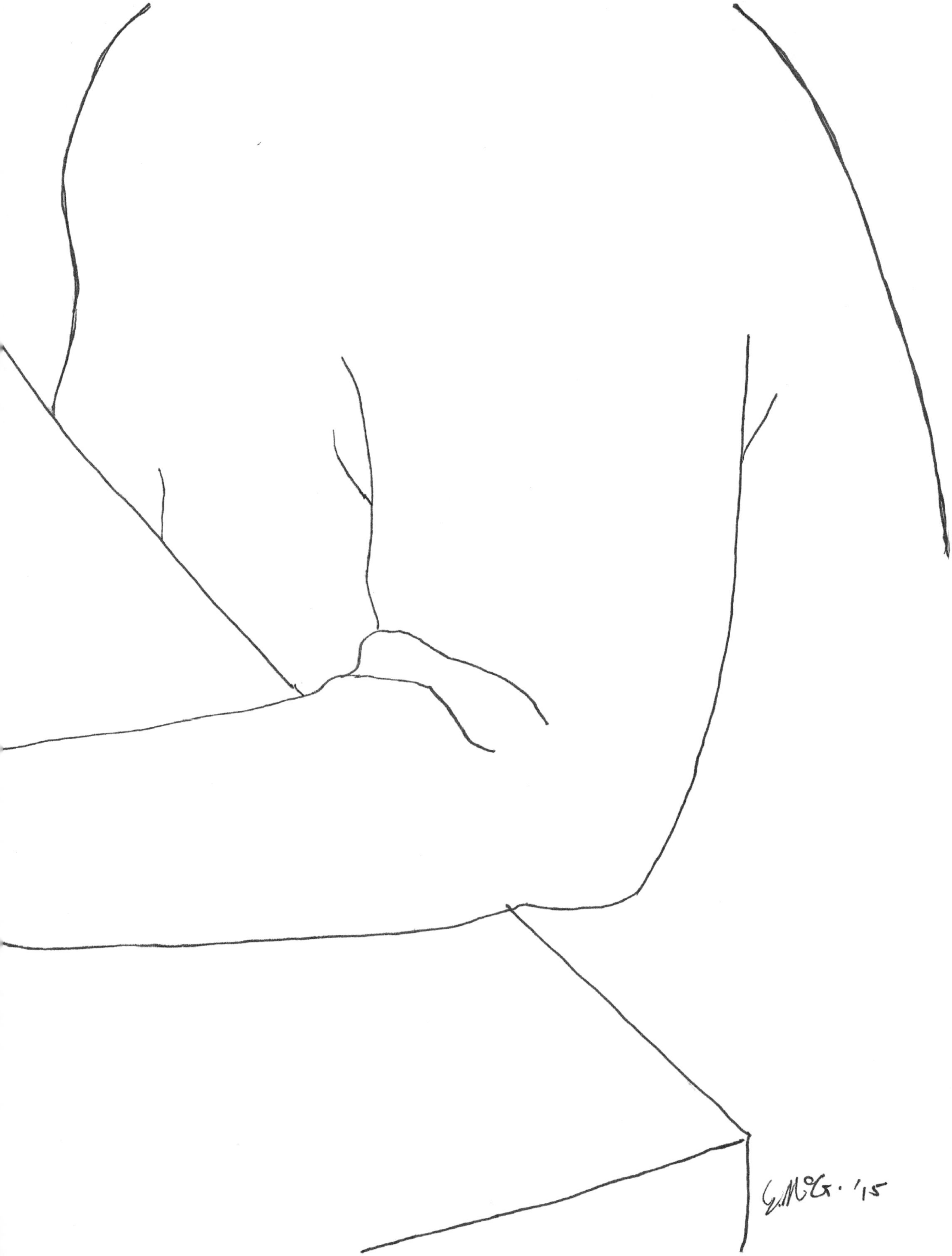
E.McG. '15

Julie Mehretu

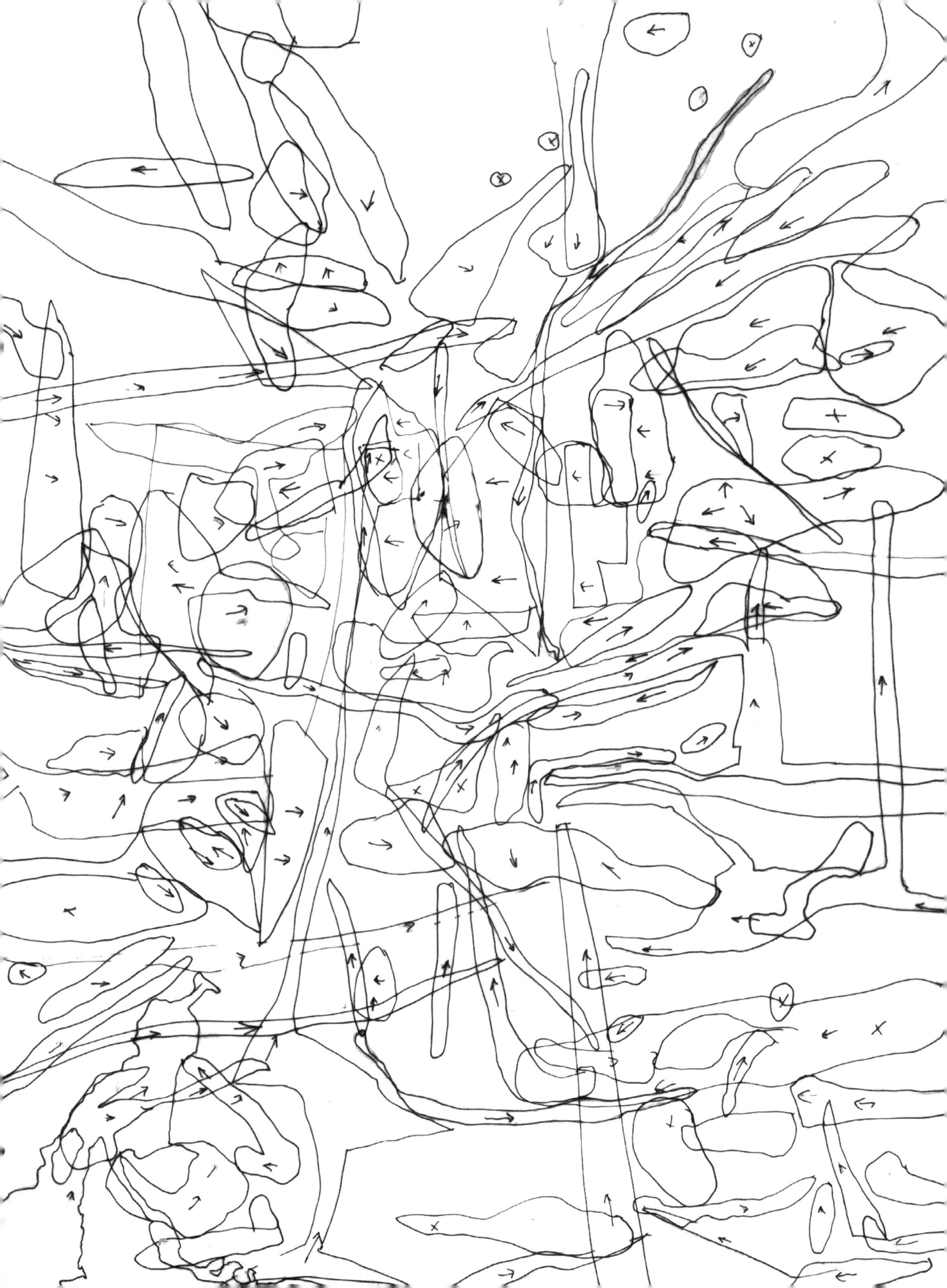

Malcolm Morley

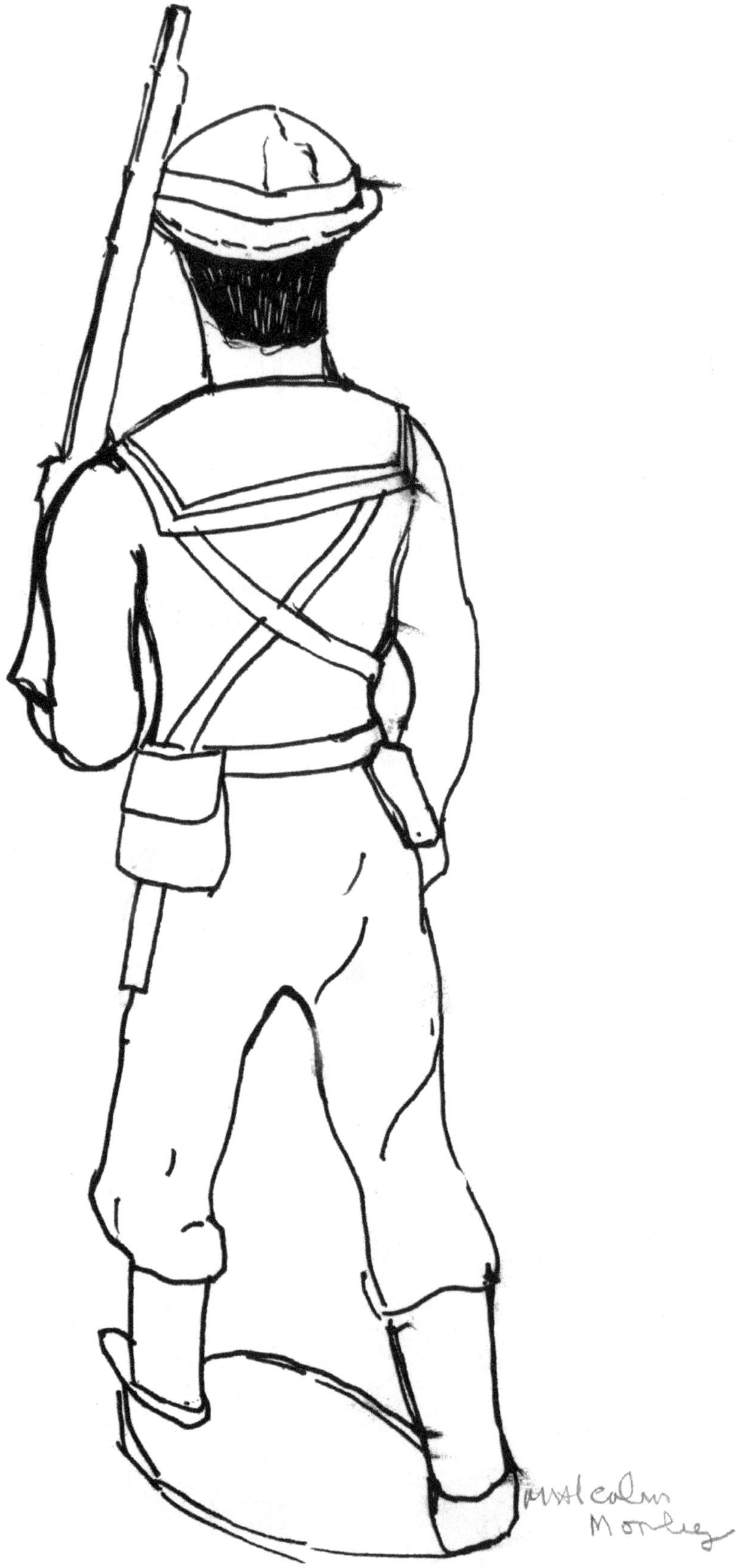

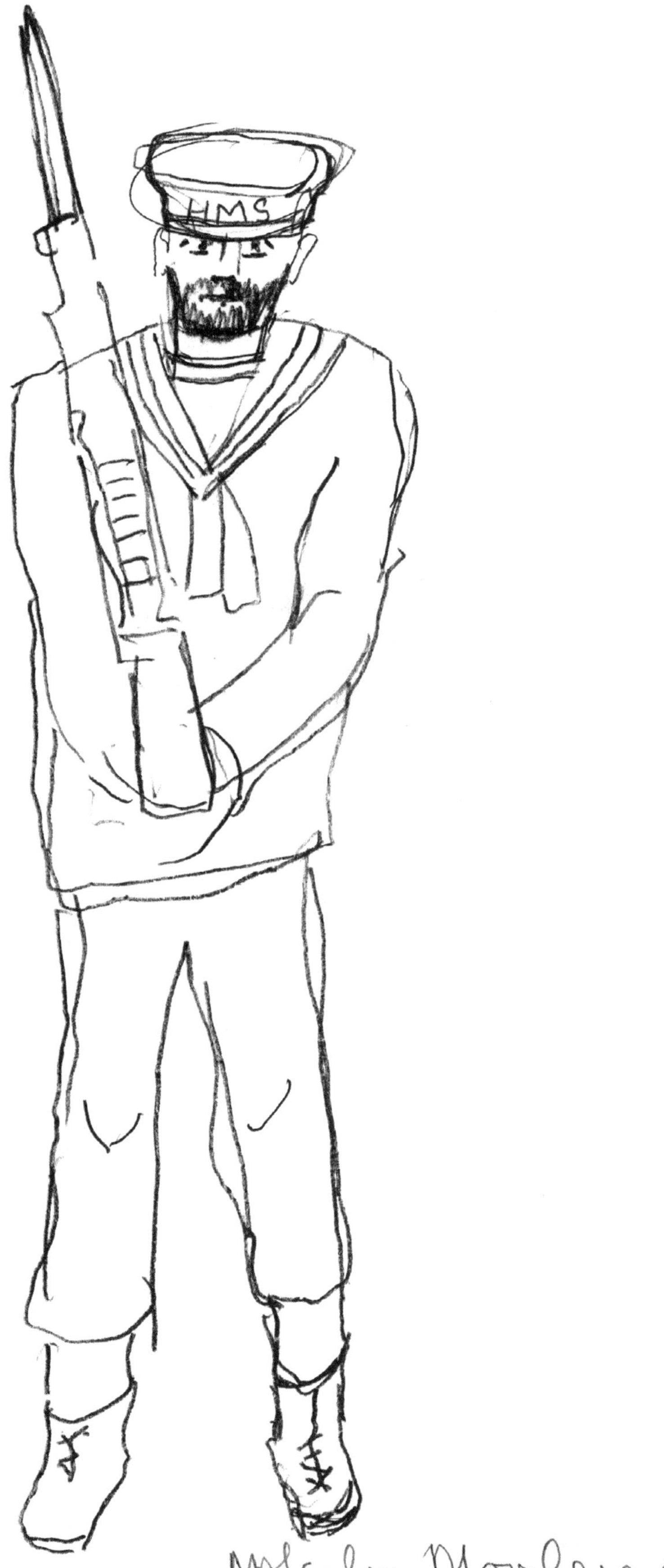
HMS
Malcolm Morley

Kambui Olujimi

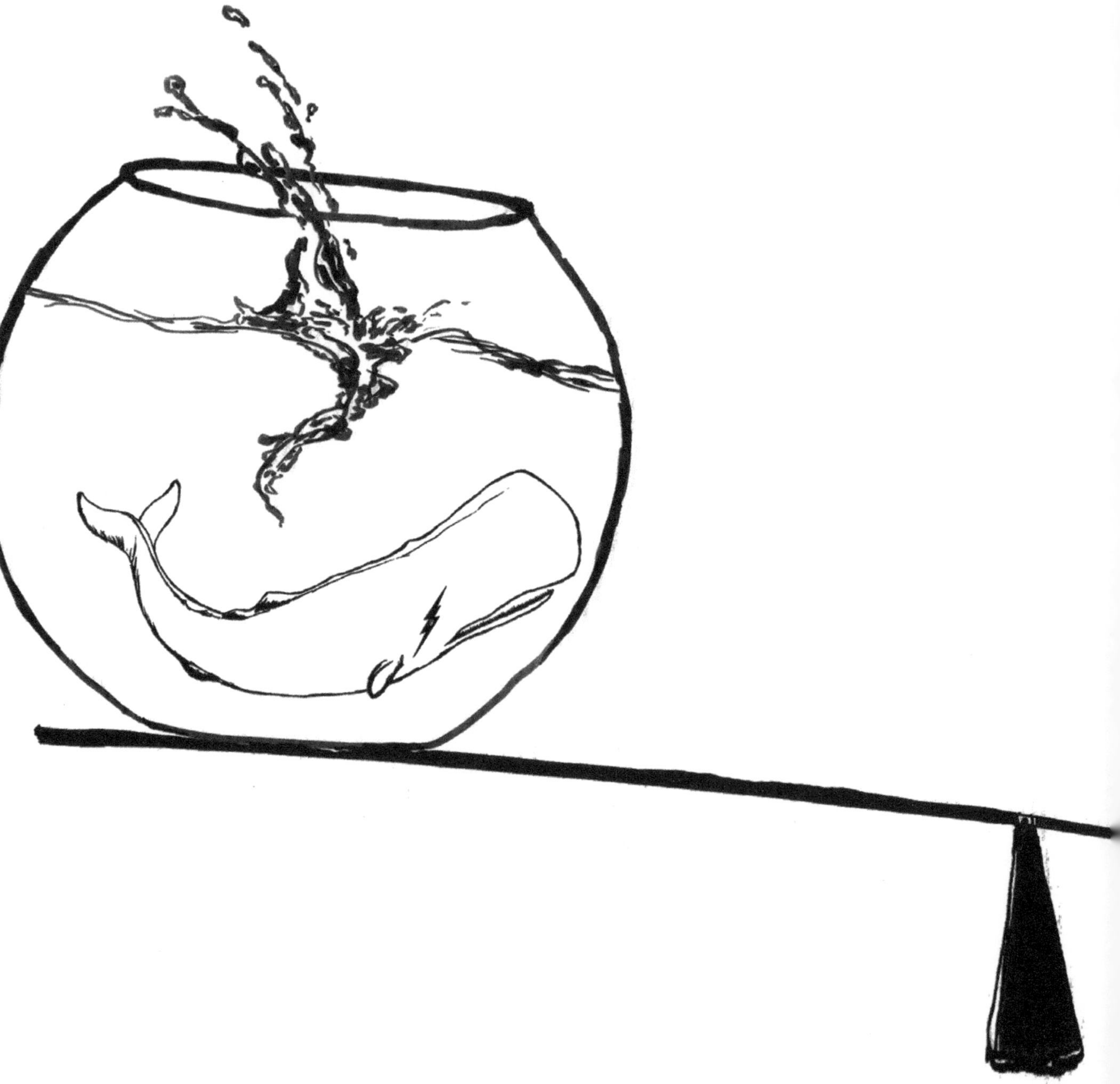

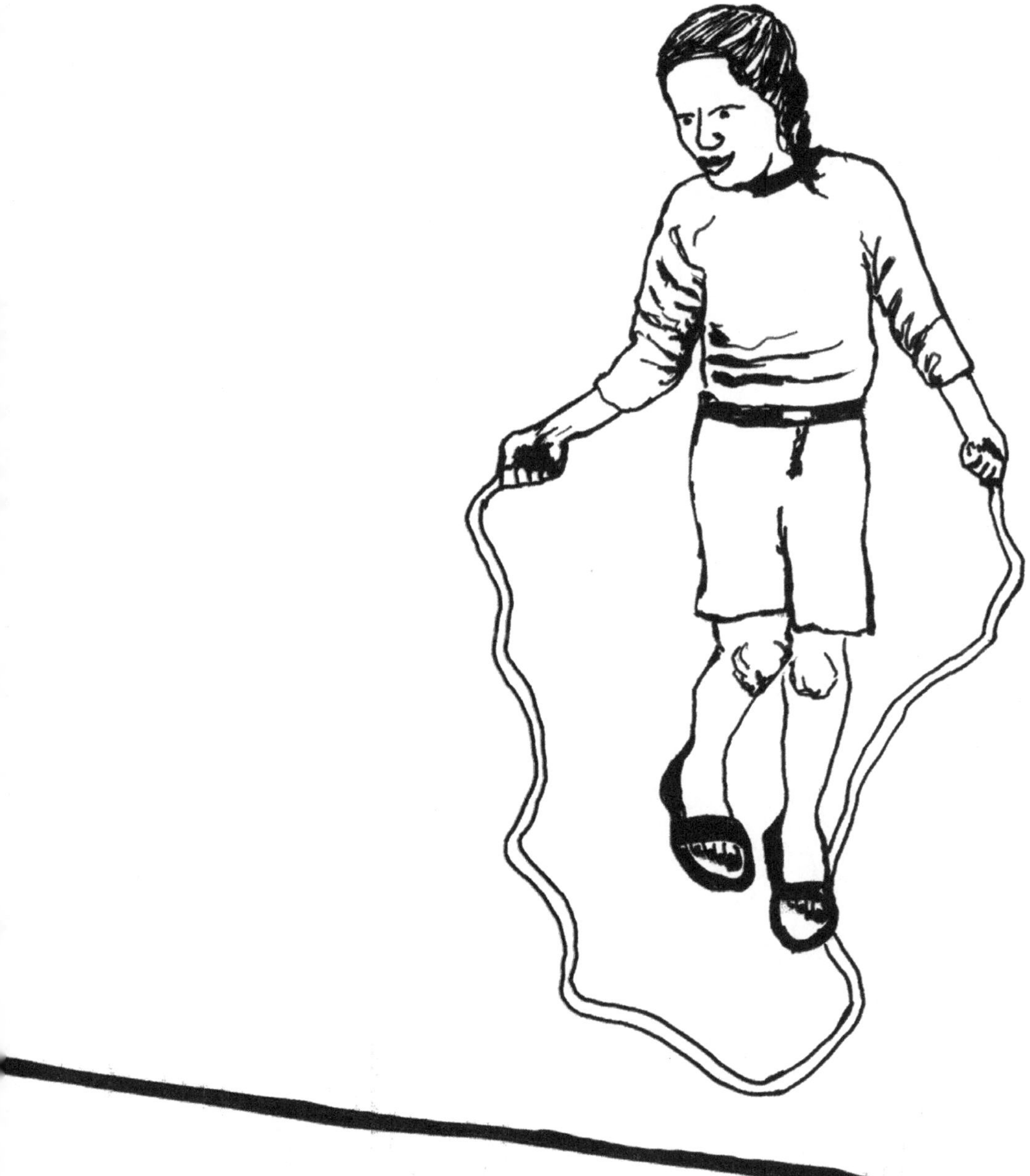

Angel Otero

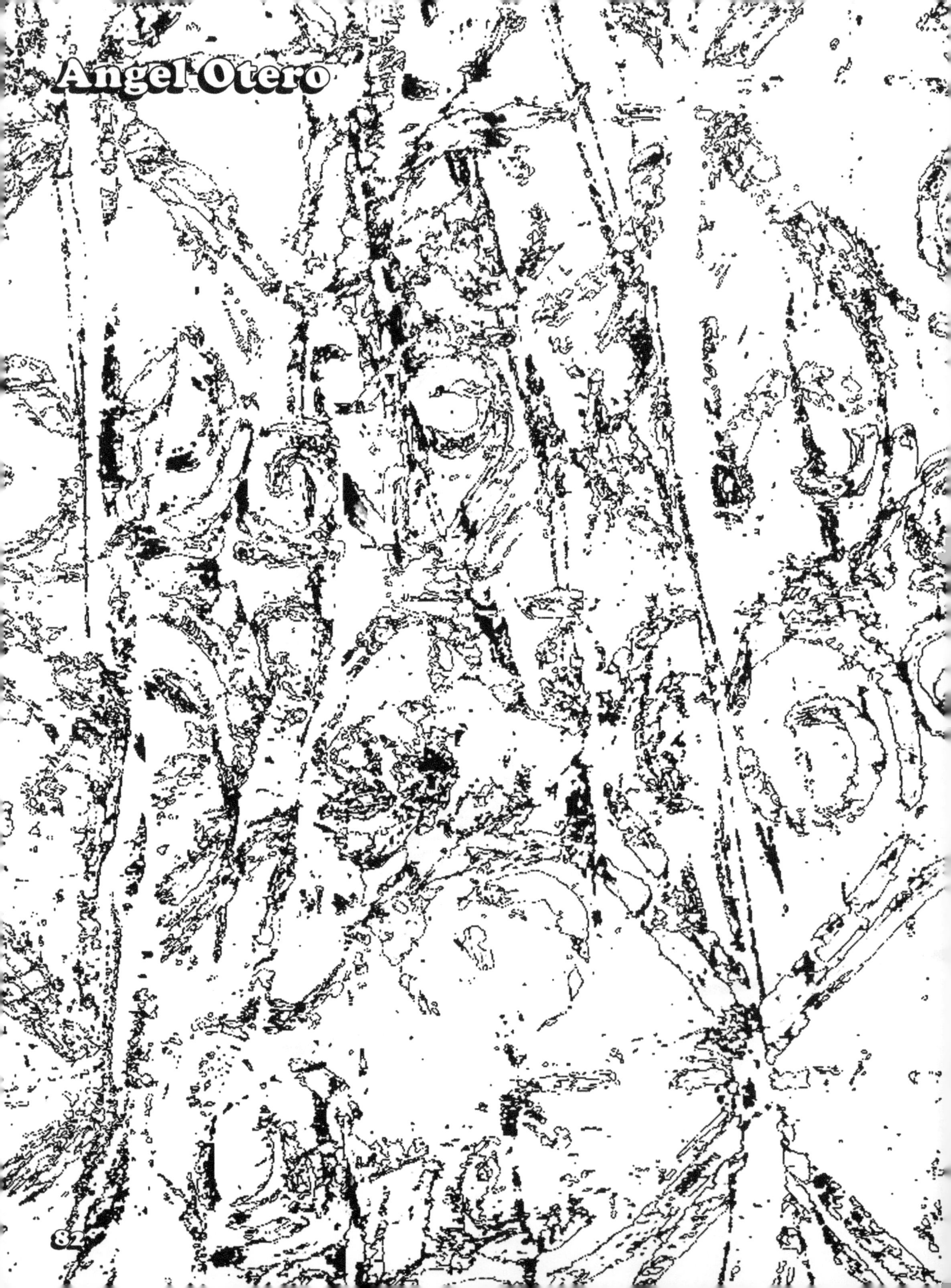

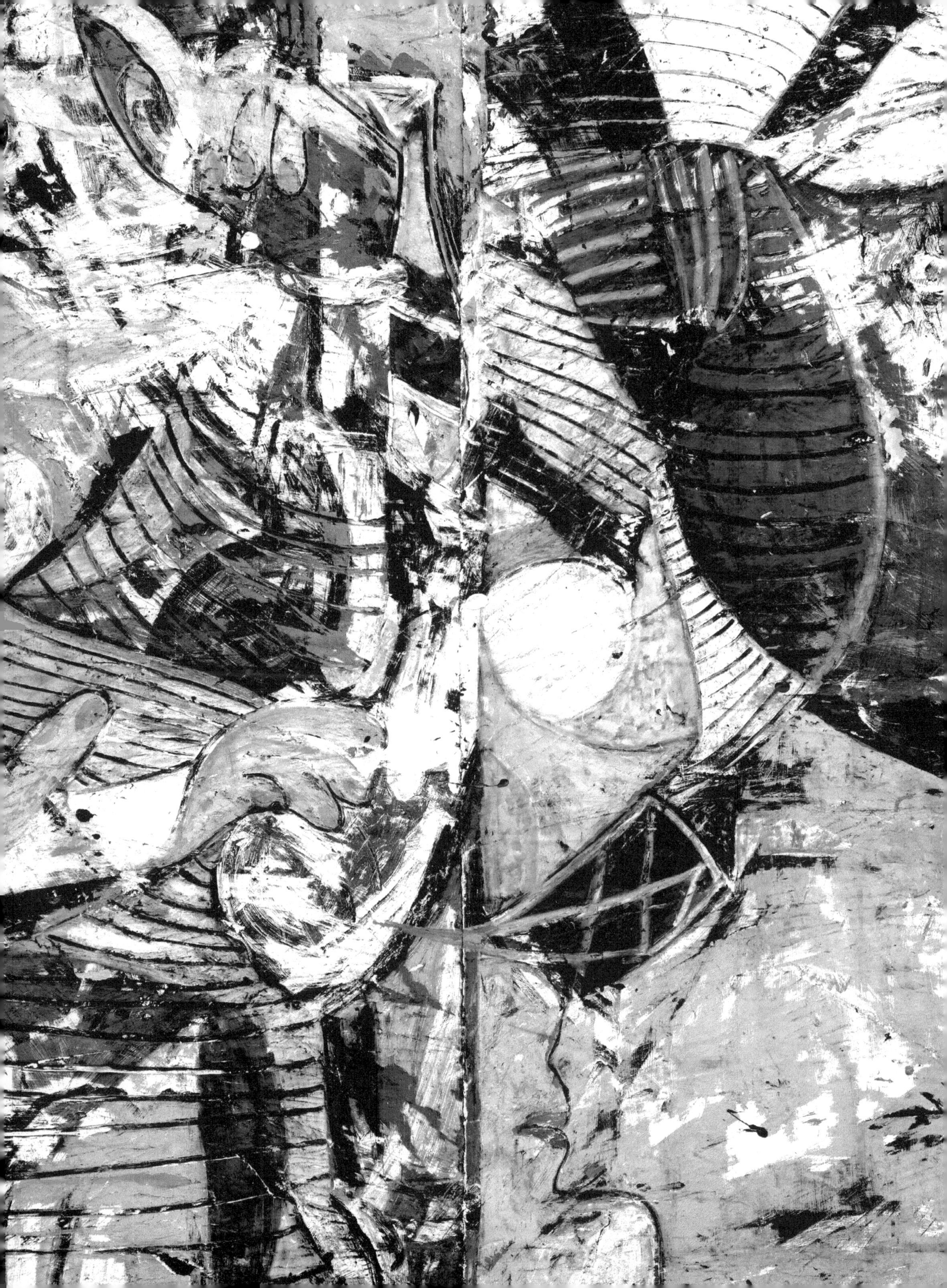

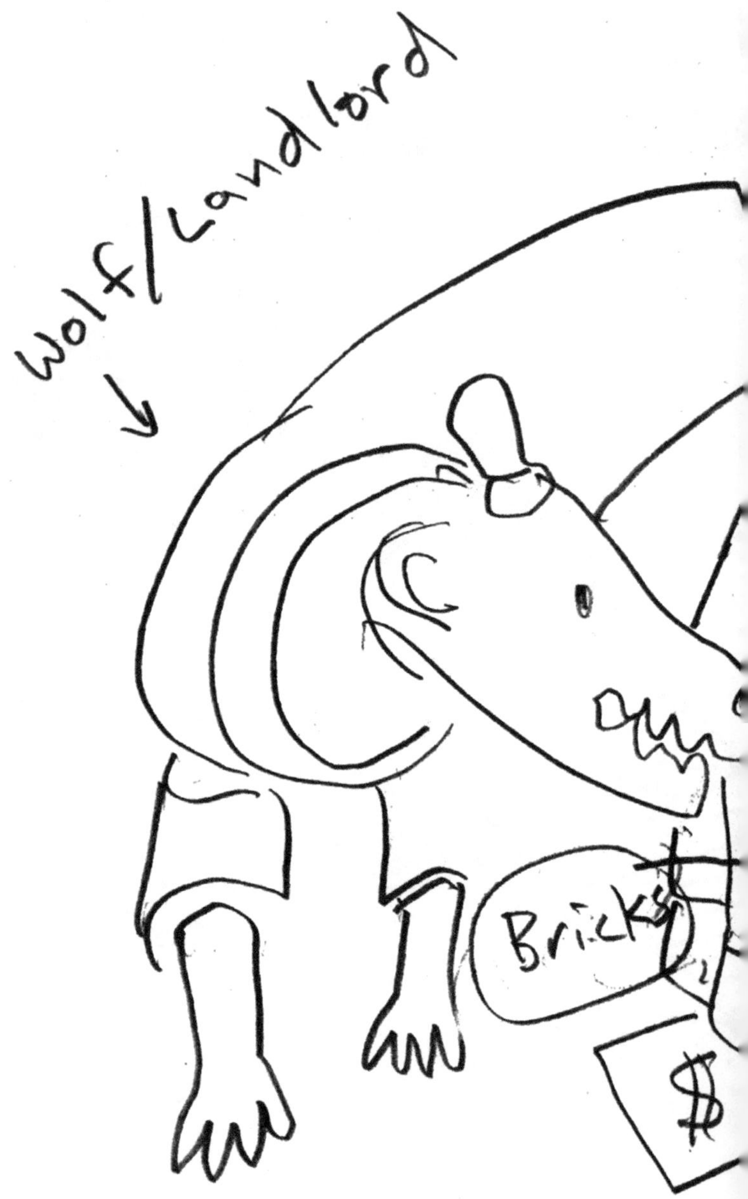

THREE LITTLE PIGS

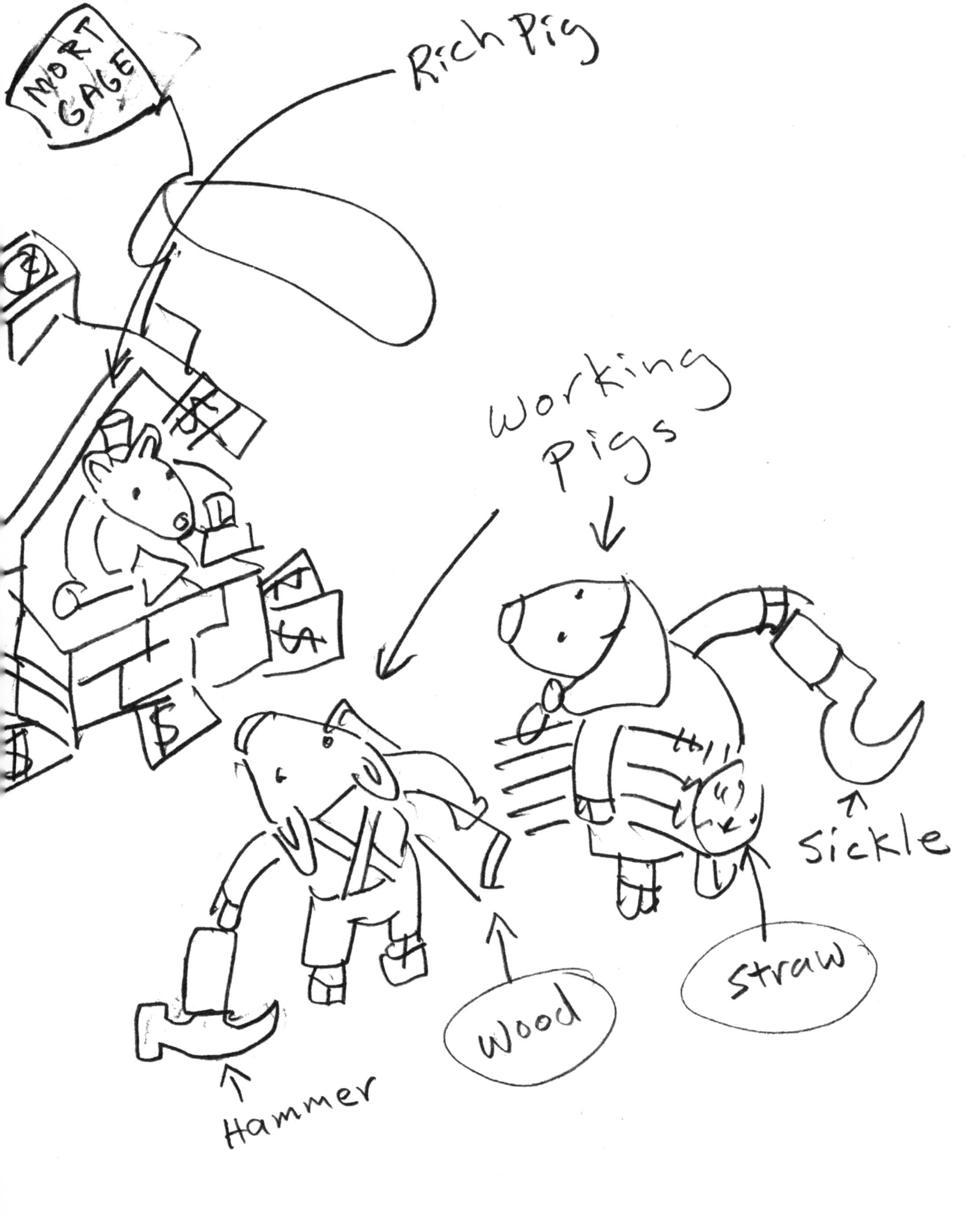

MORT GAGE
Rich Pig
Working Pigs
$
Sickle
Straw
Wood
Hammer

Erik Parker

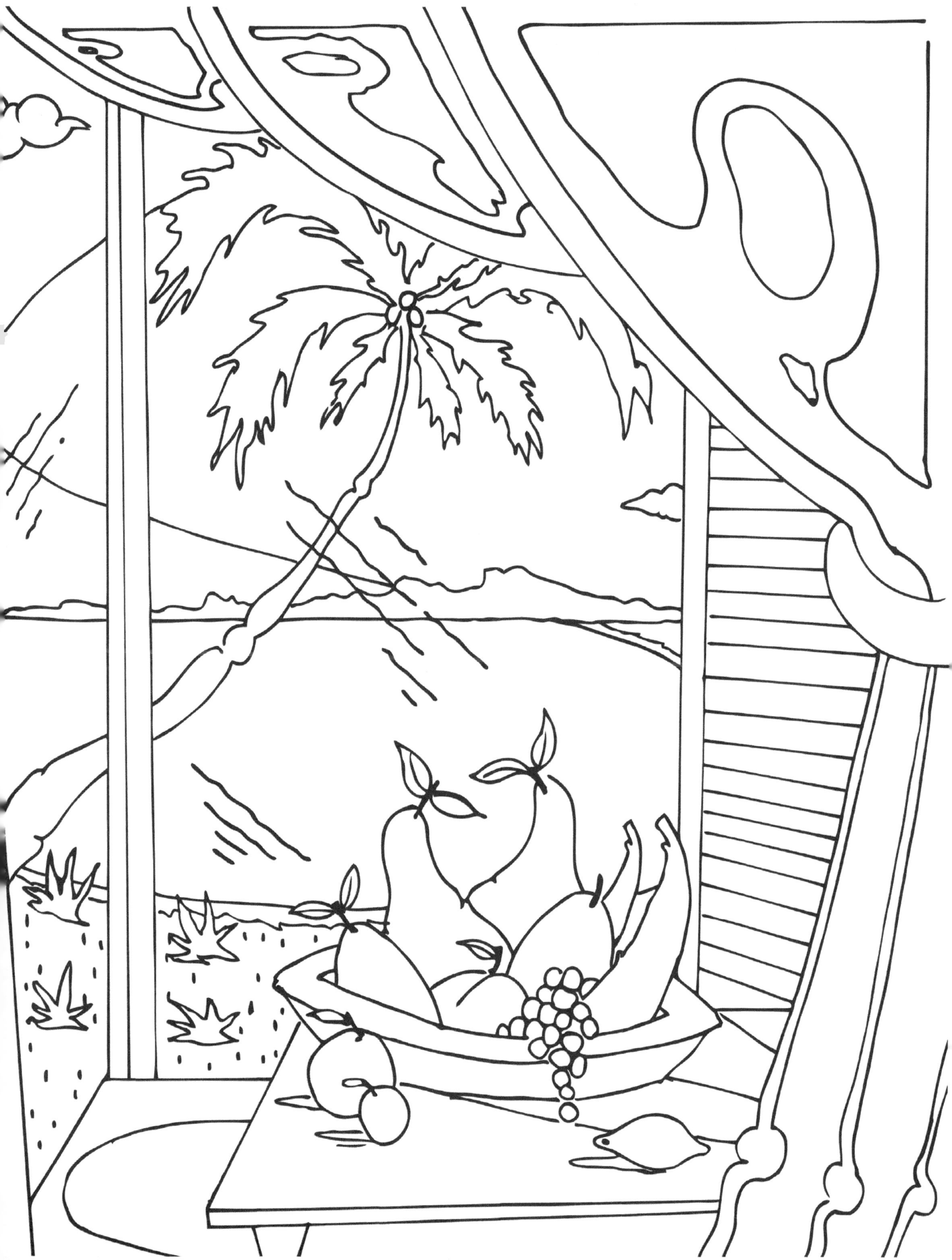

Matthew Ritchie

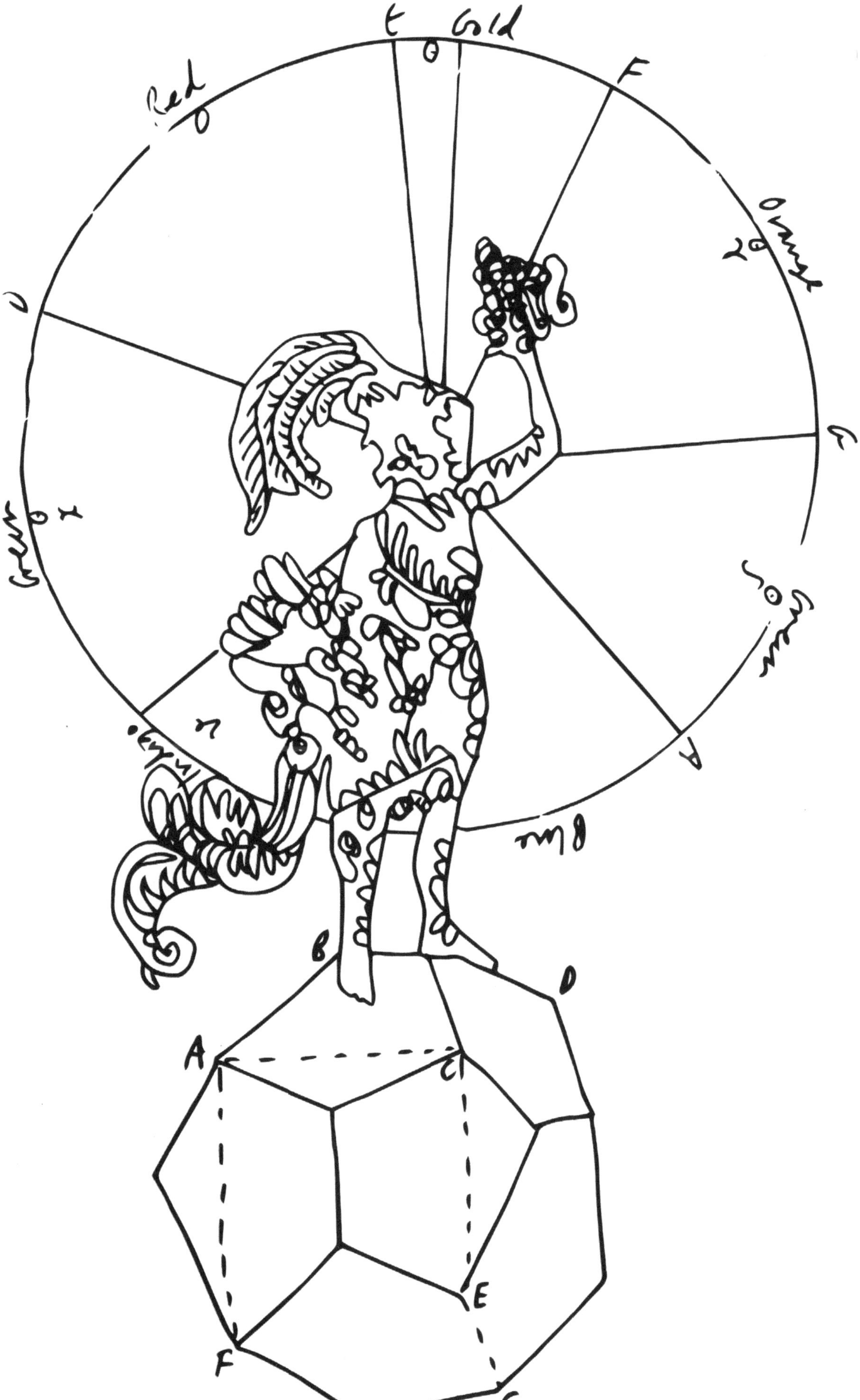
Red
Gold
Orange
Green
Blue
A
B
C
D
E
F
G

Alexis Rockman

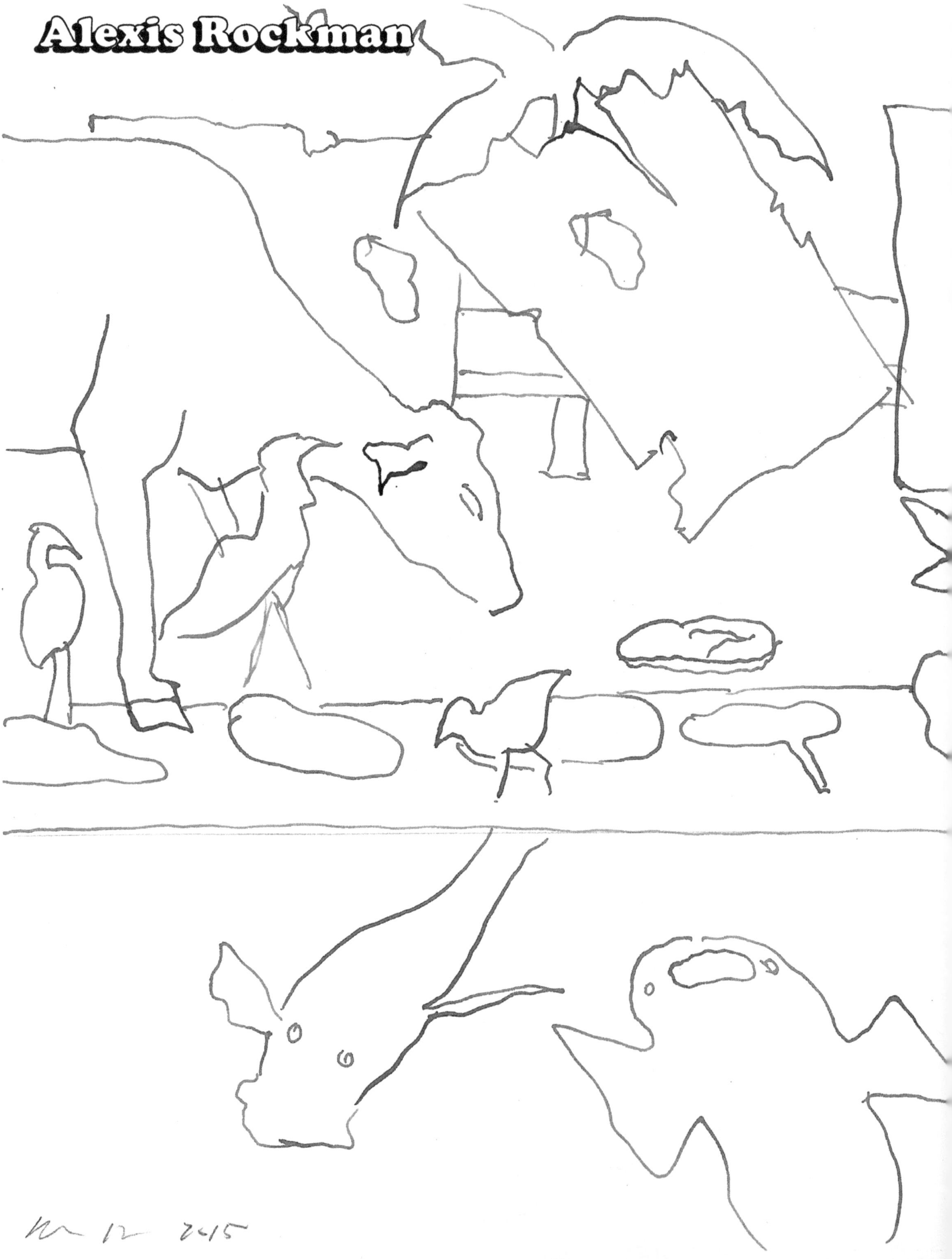

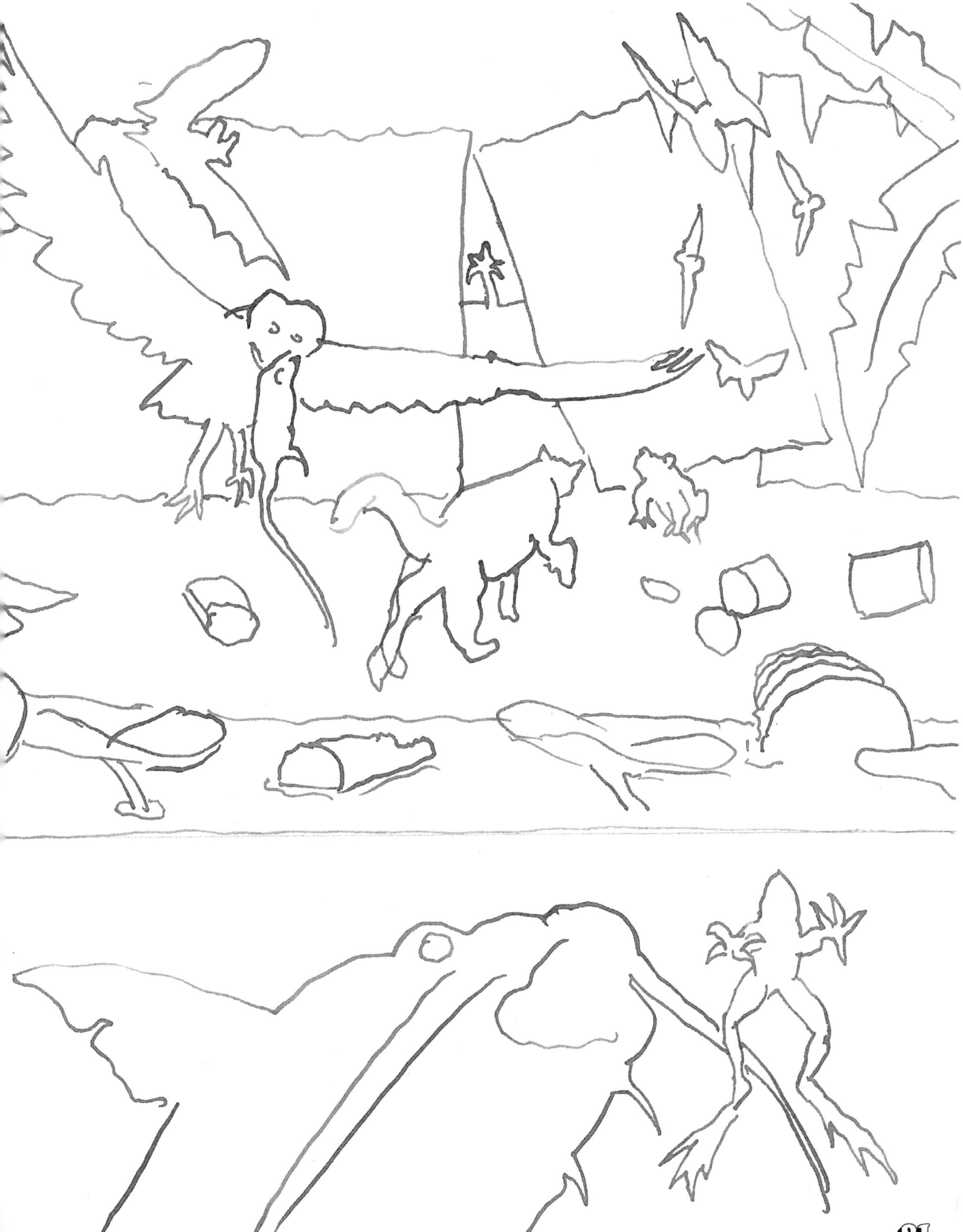

Ugo Rondinone

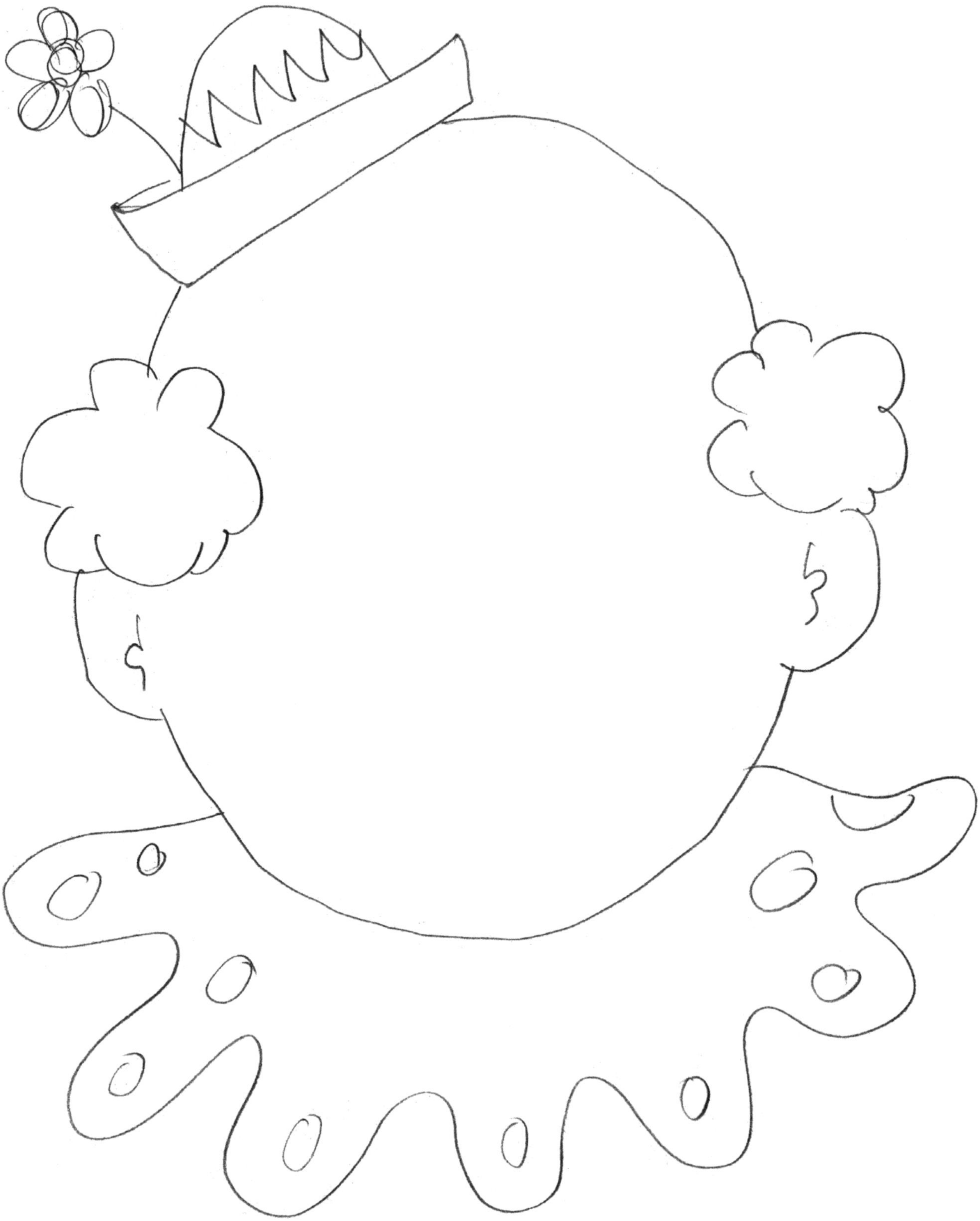

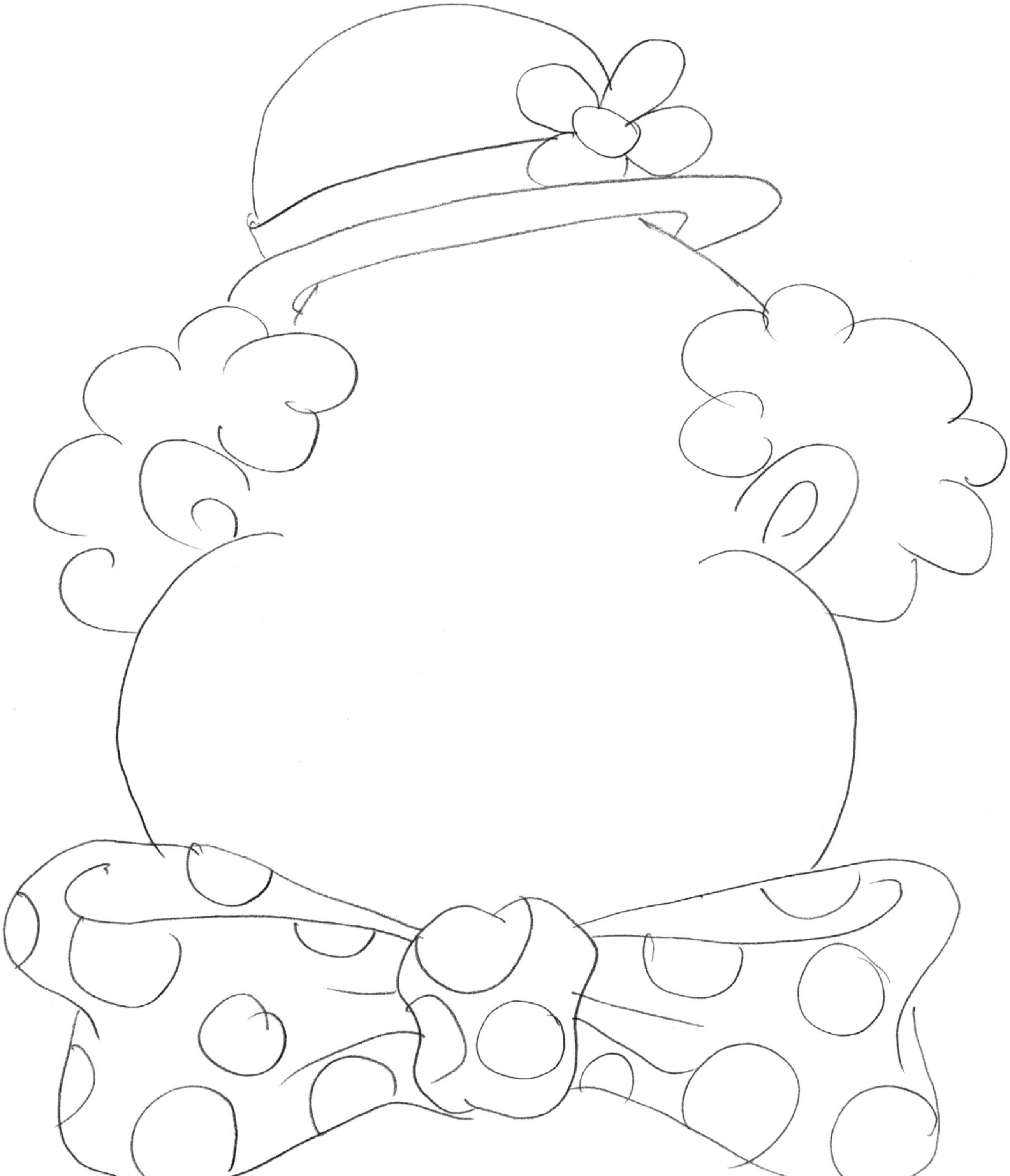

Kenny Scharf

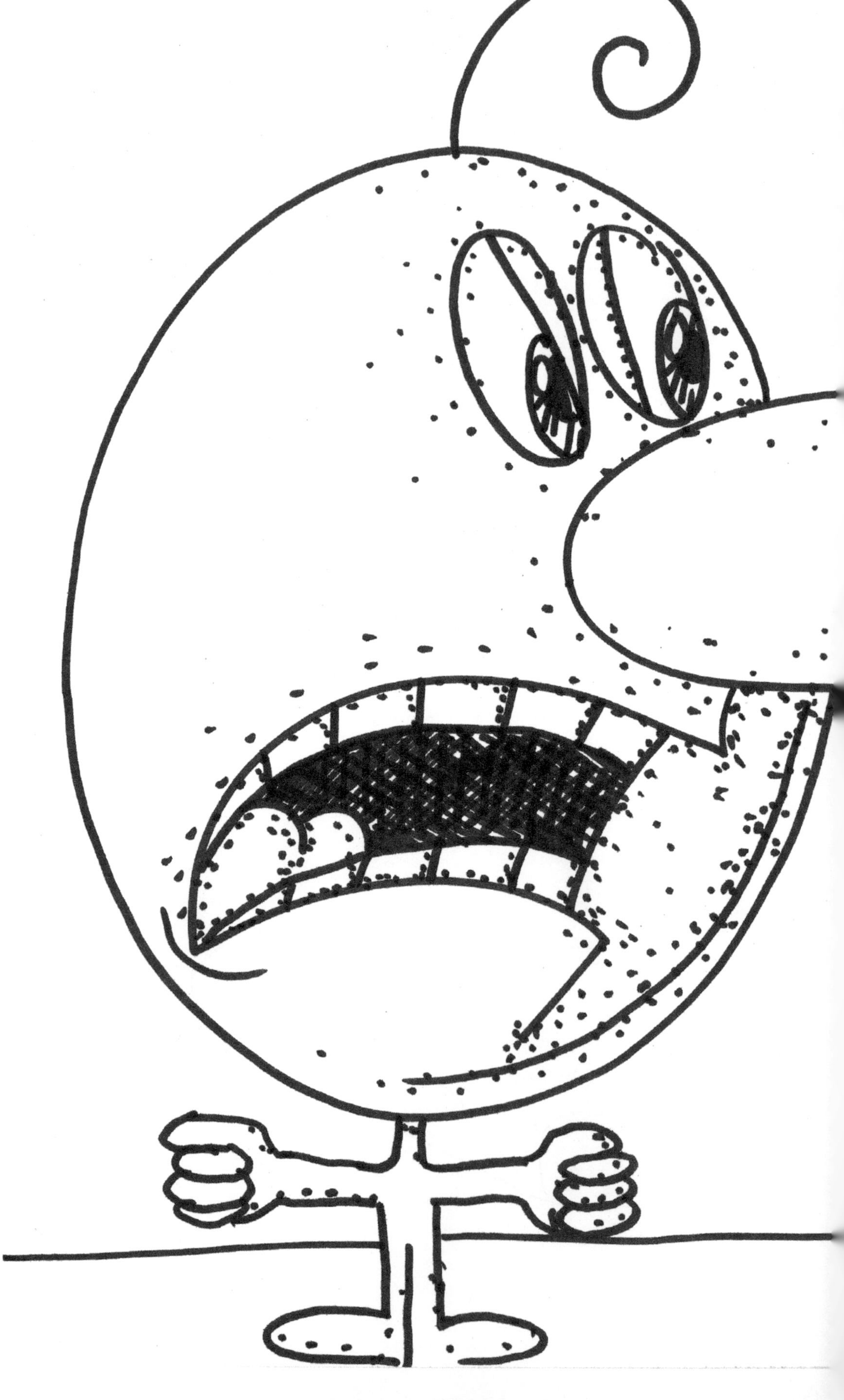

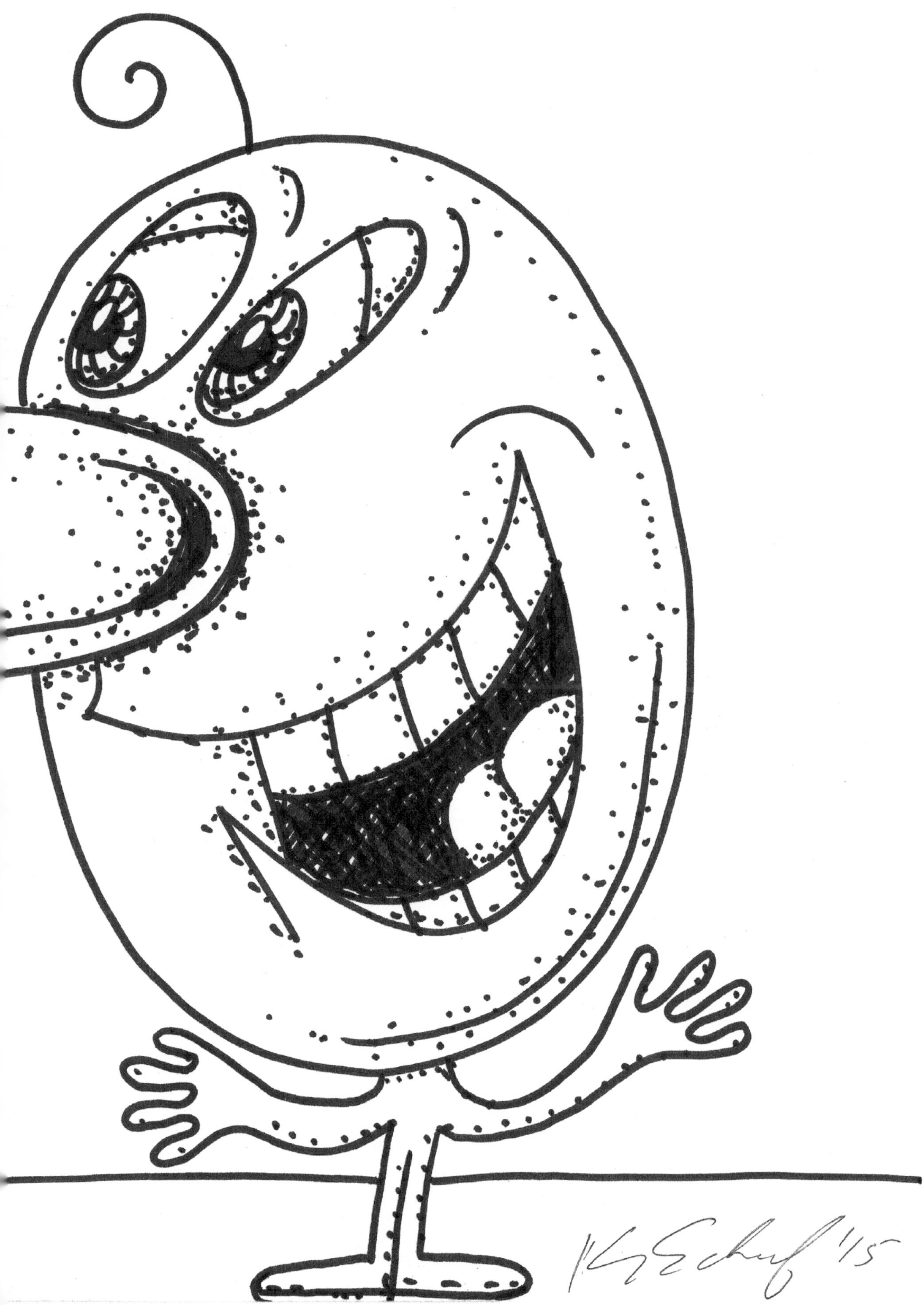

Andrew Sendor

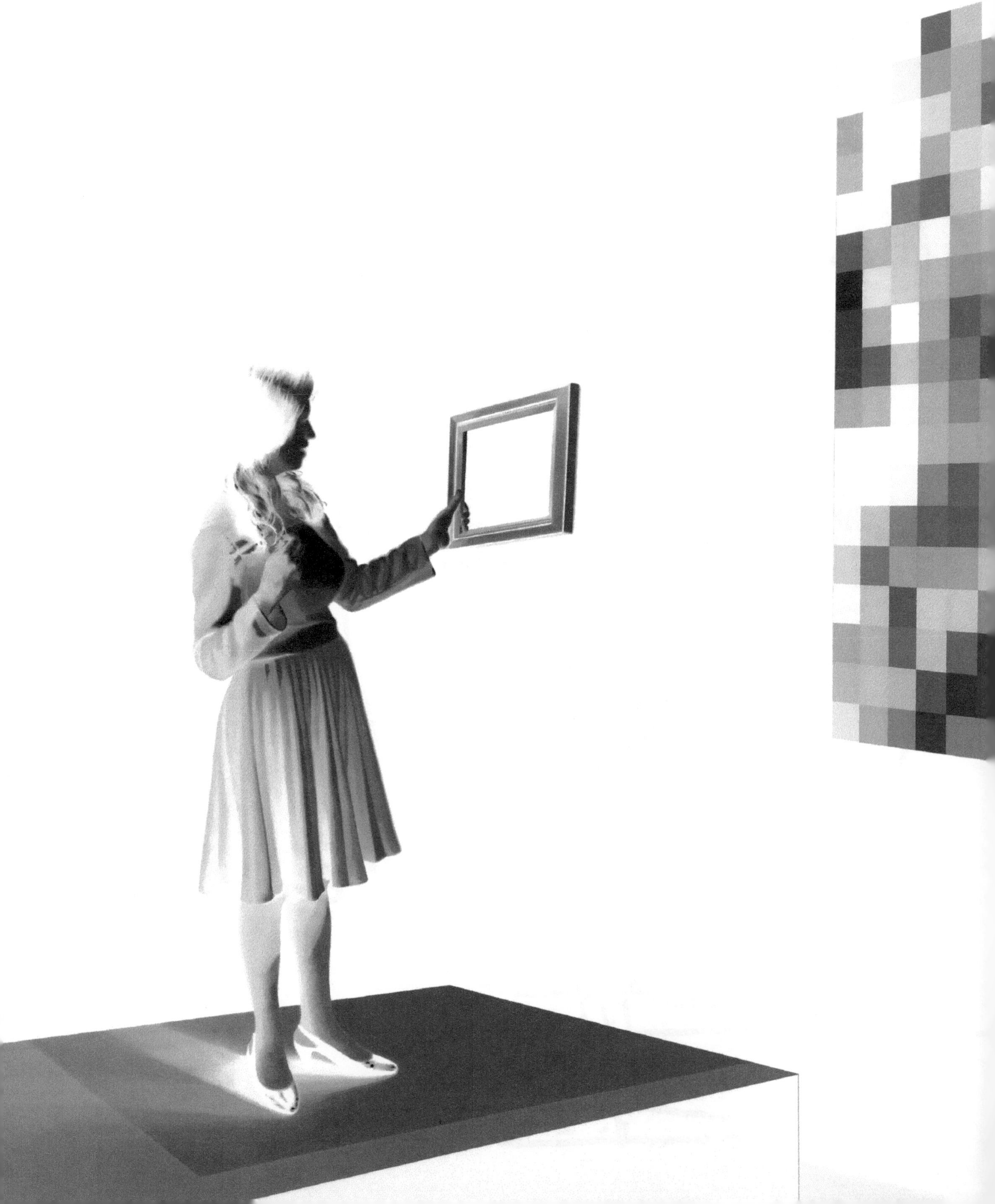

Alyson Shotz

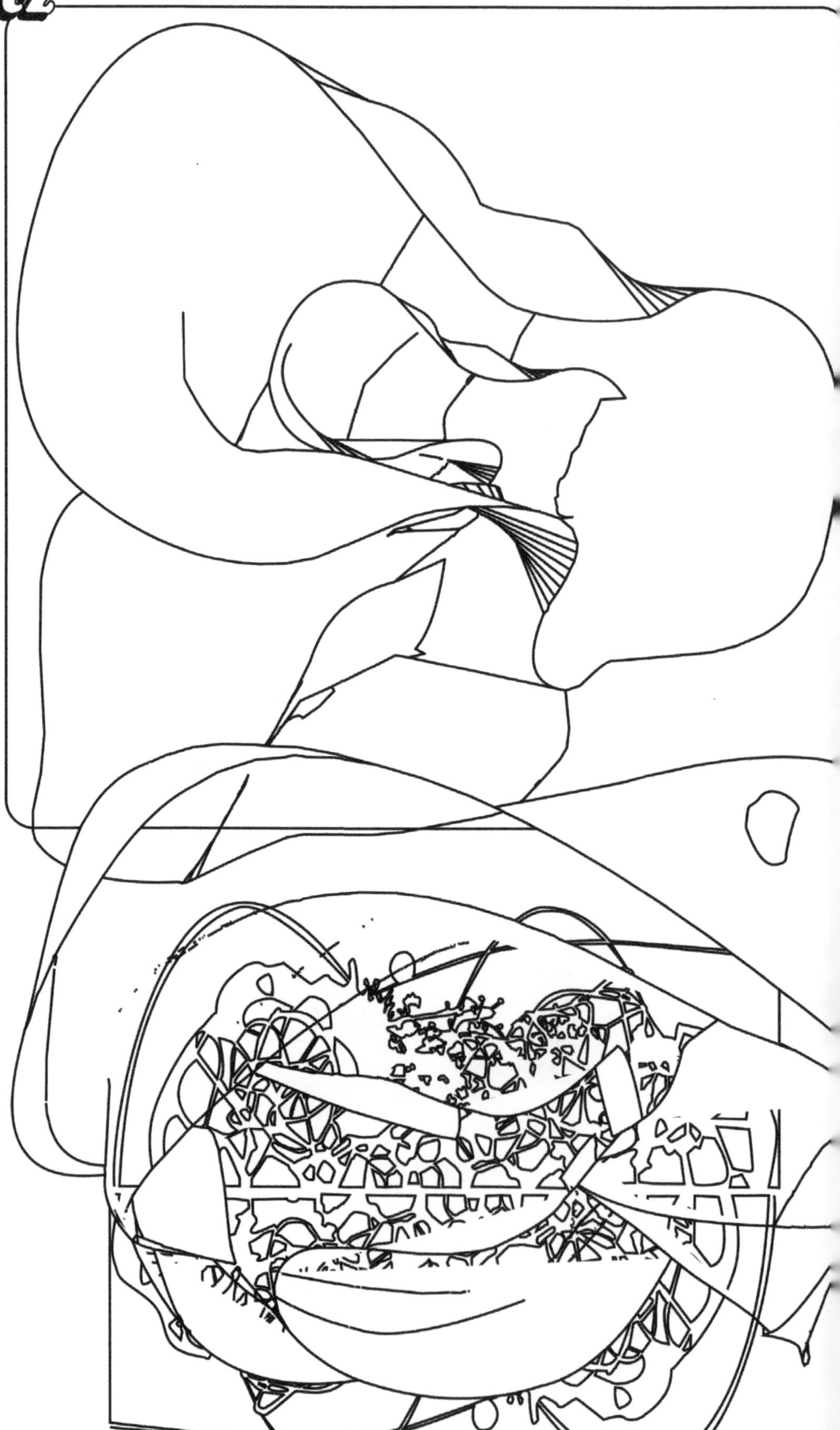

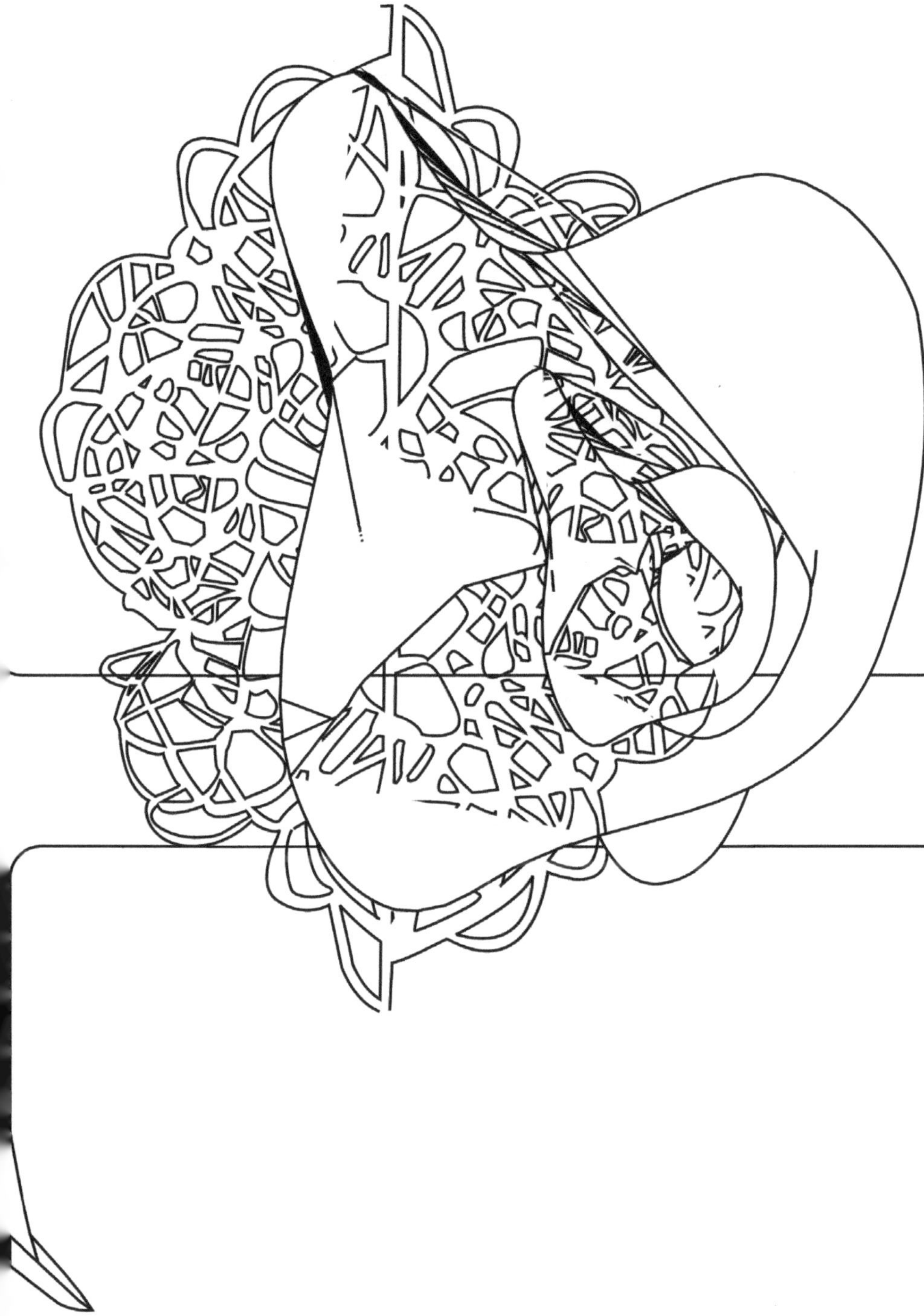

A.Shotz 2015

Tom Slaughter

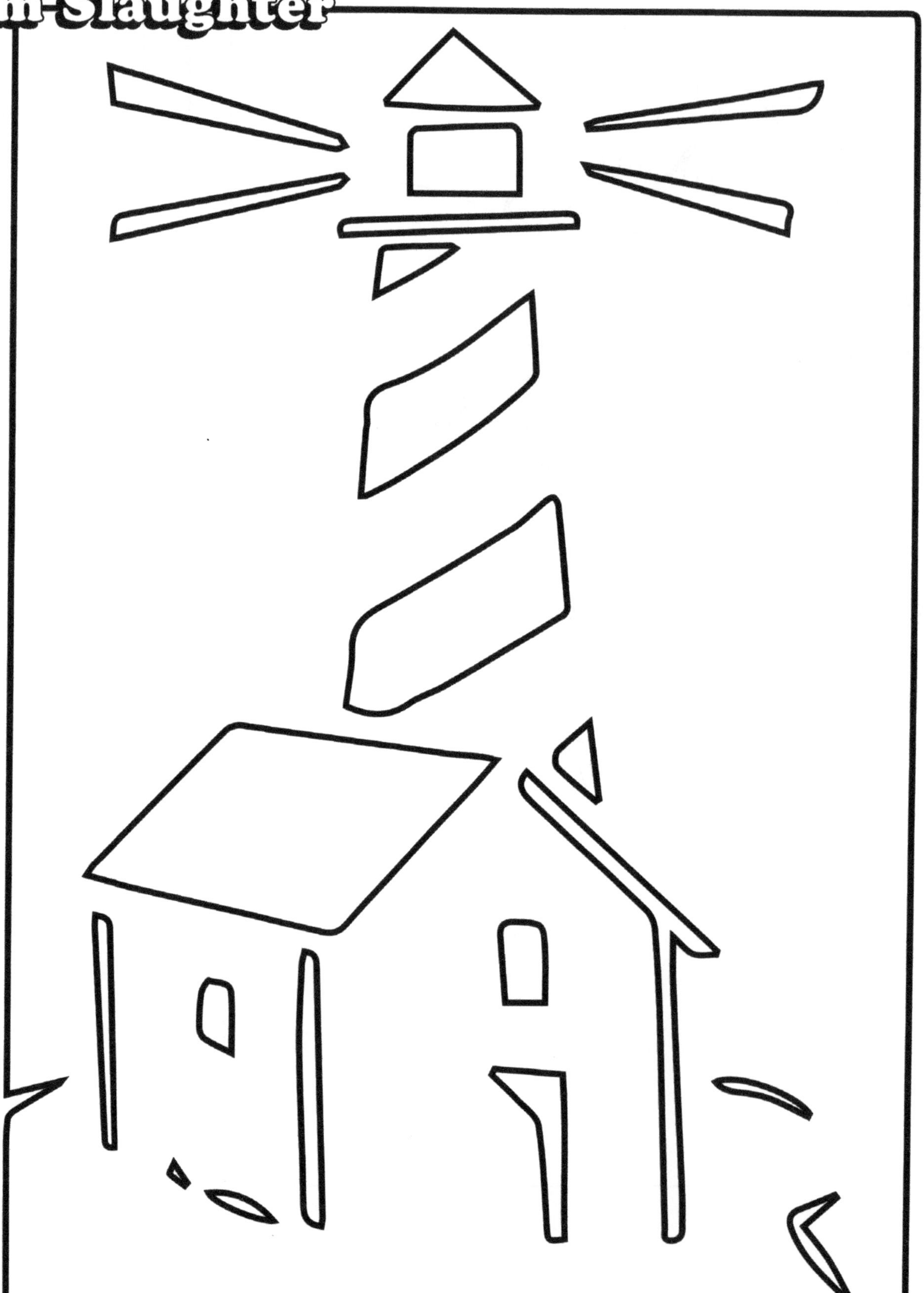

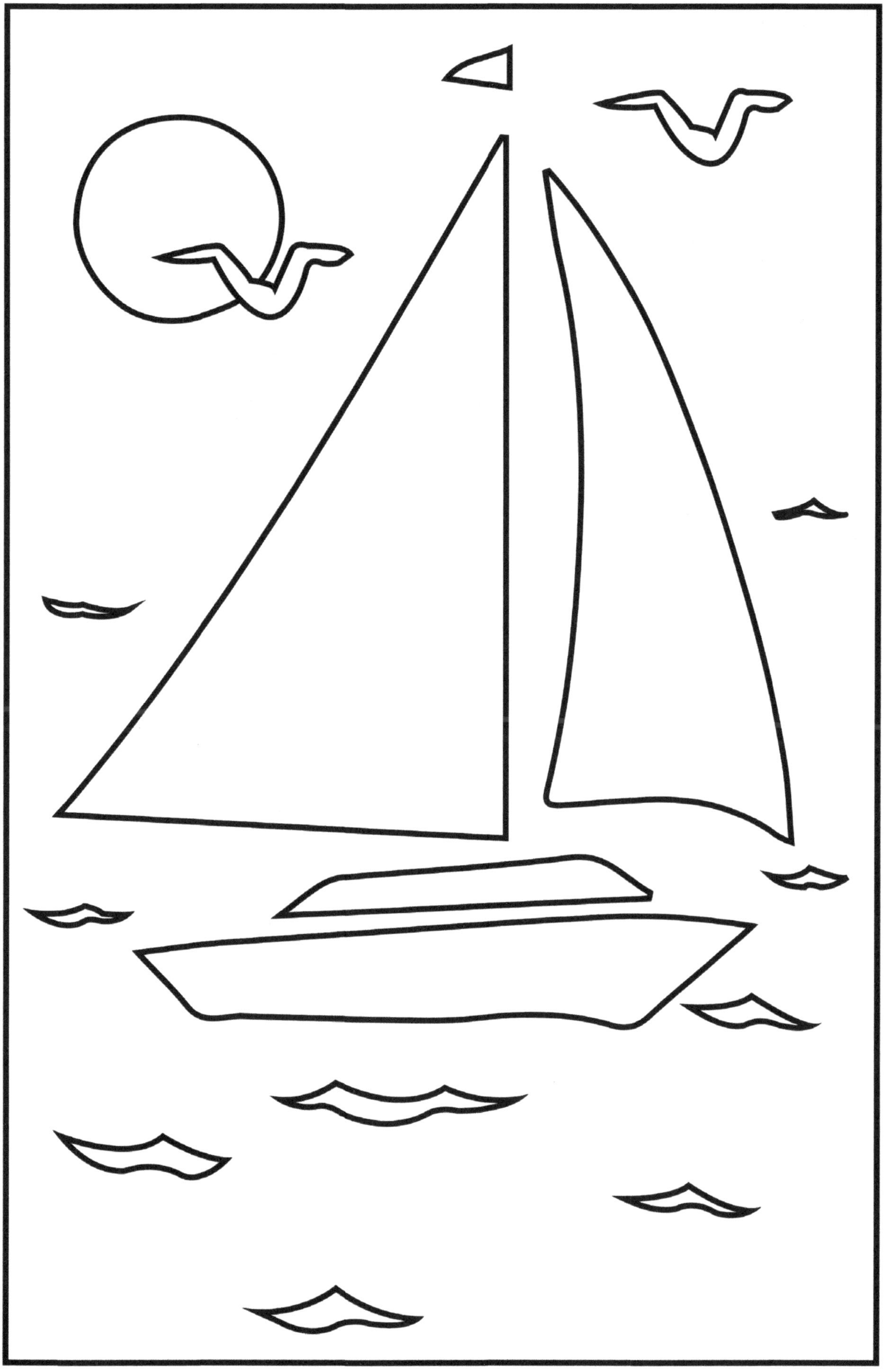

Josh Smith

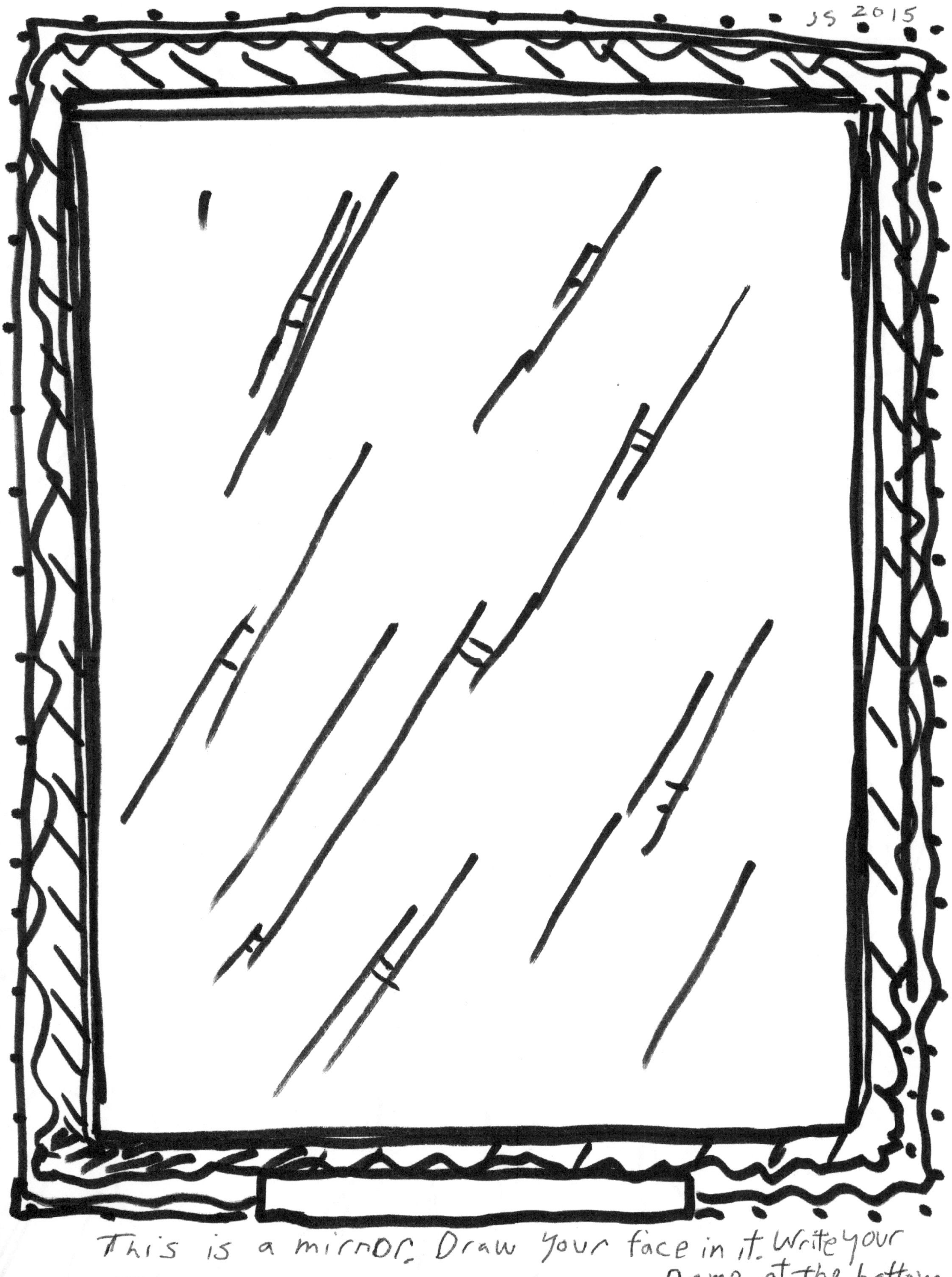

This is a mirror. Draw your face in it. Write your name at the bottom

Shinique Smith

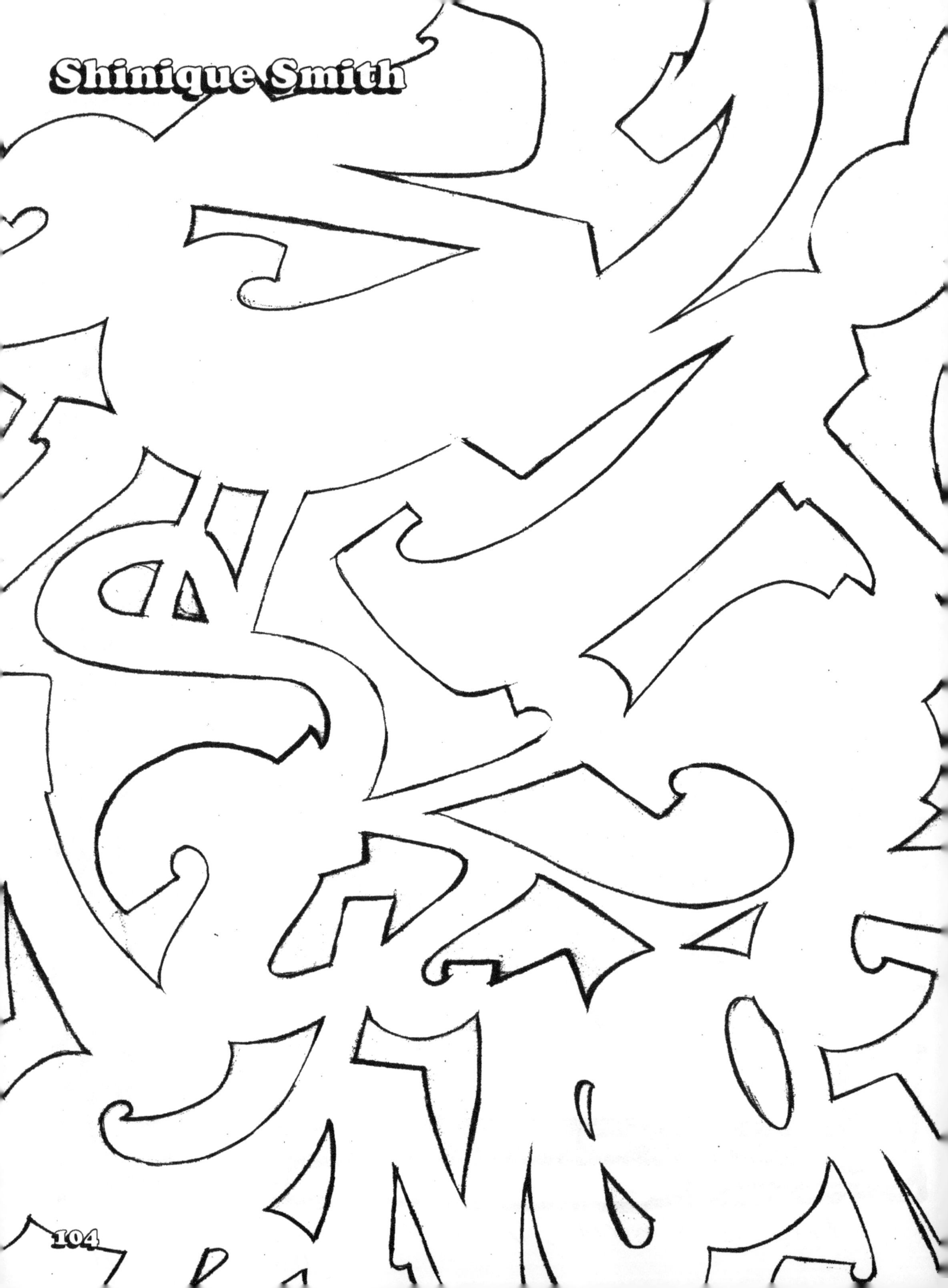

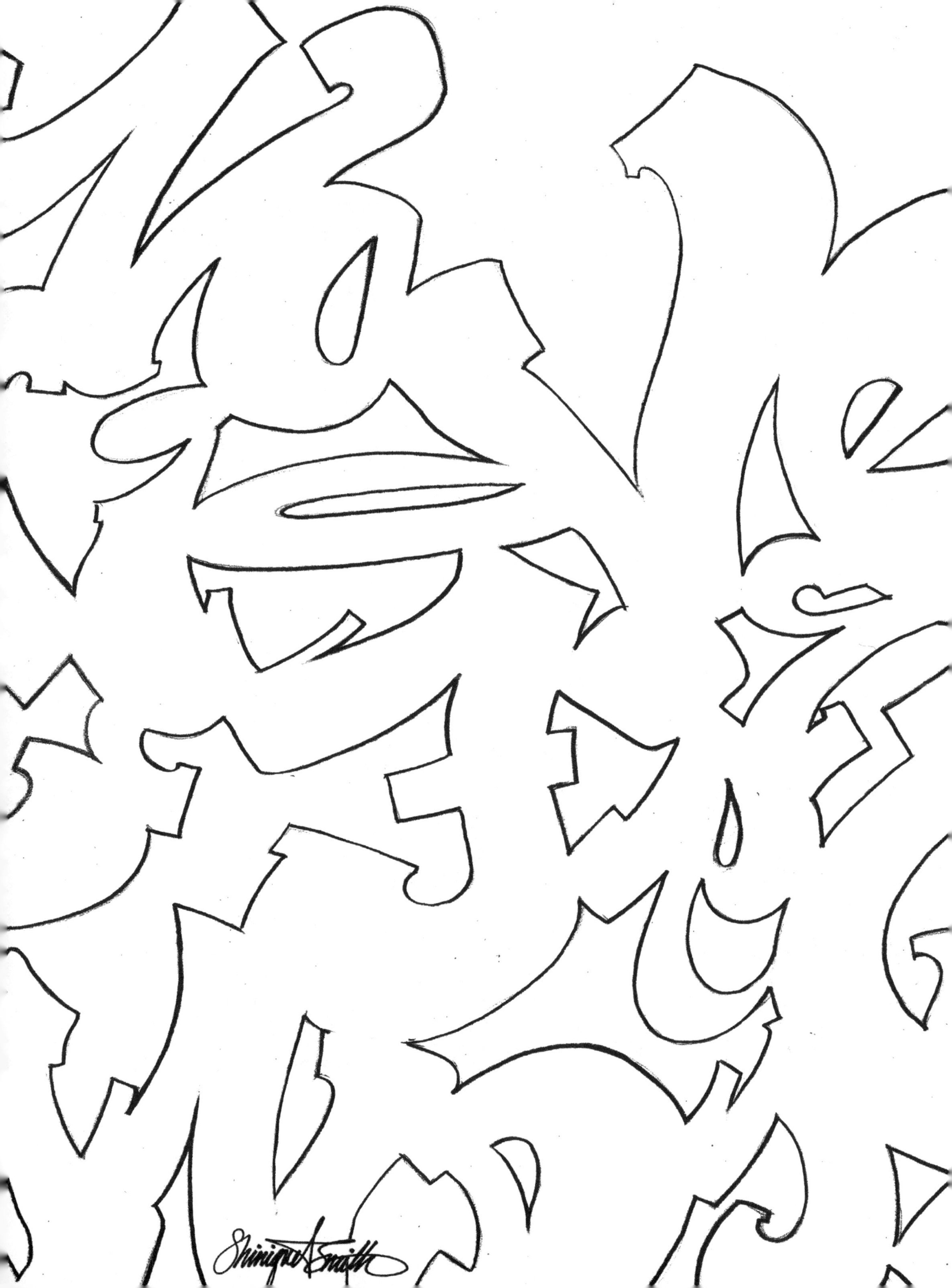
Shinique Smith

Jennifer Steinkamp

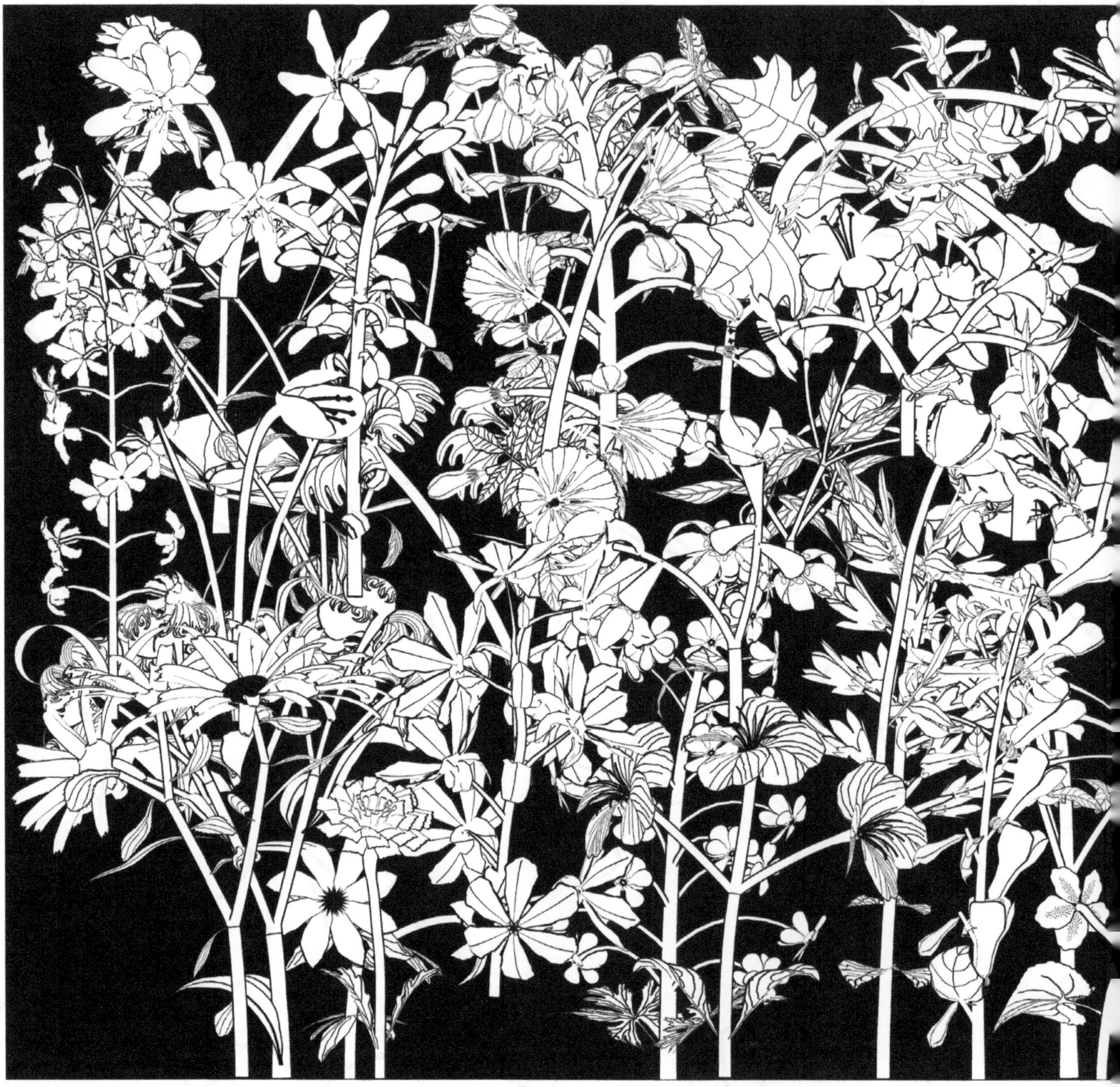

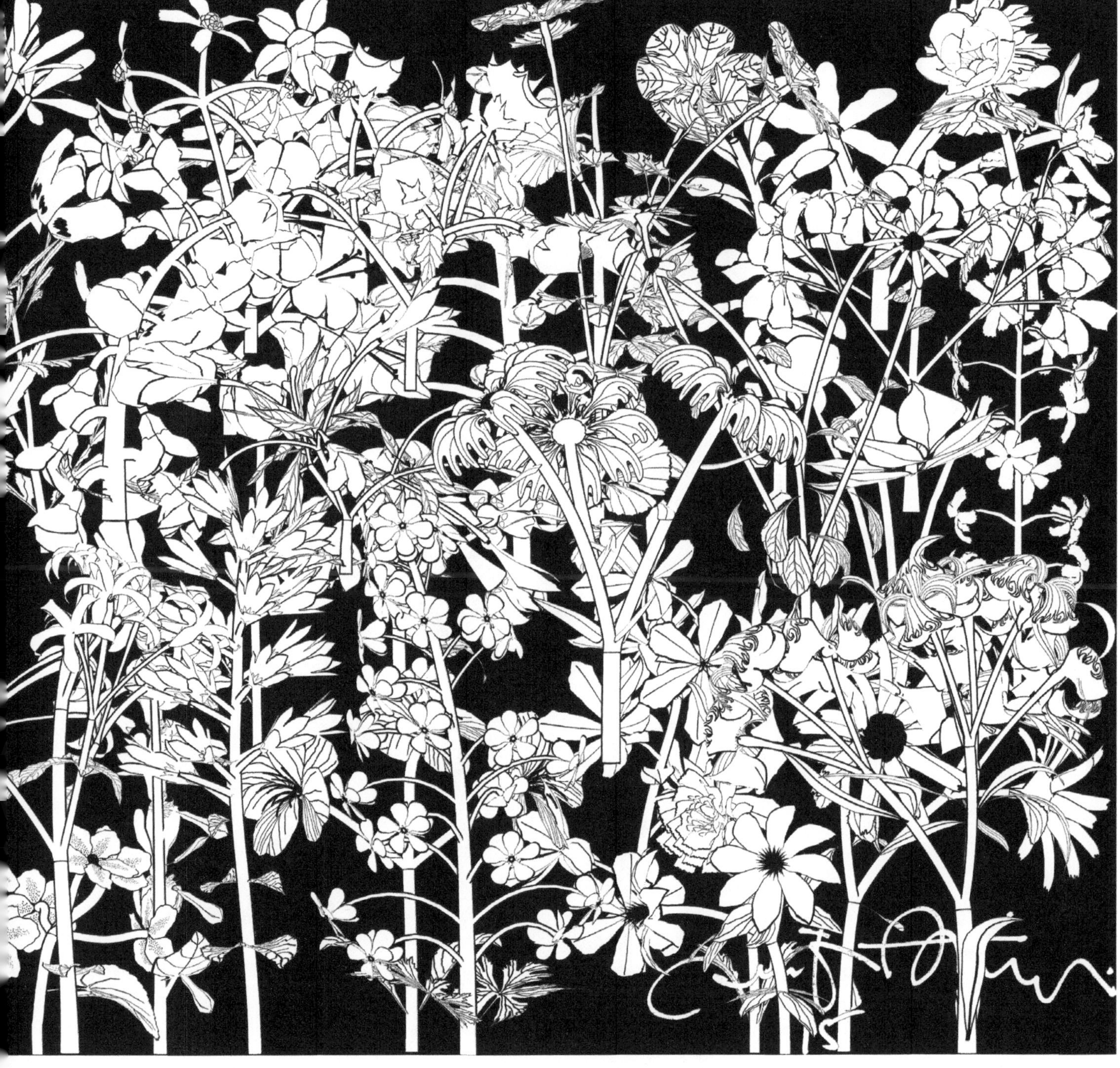

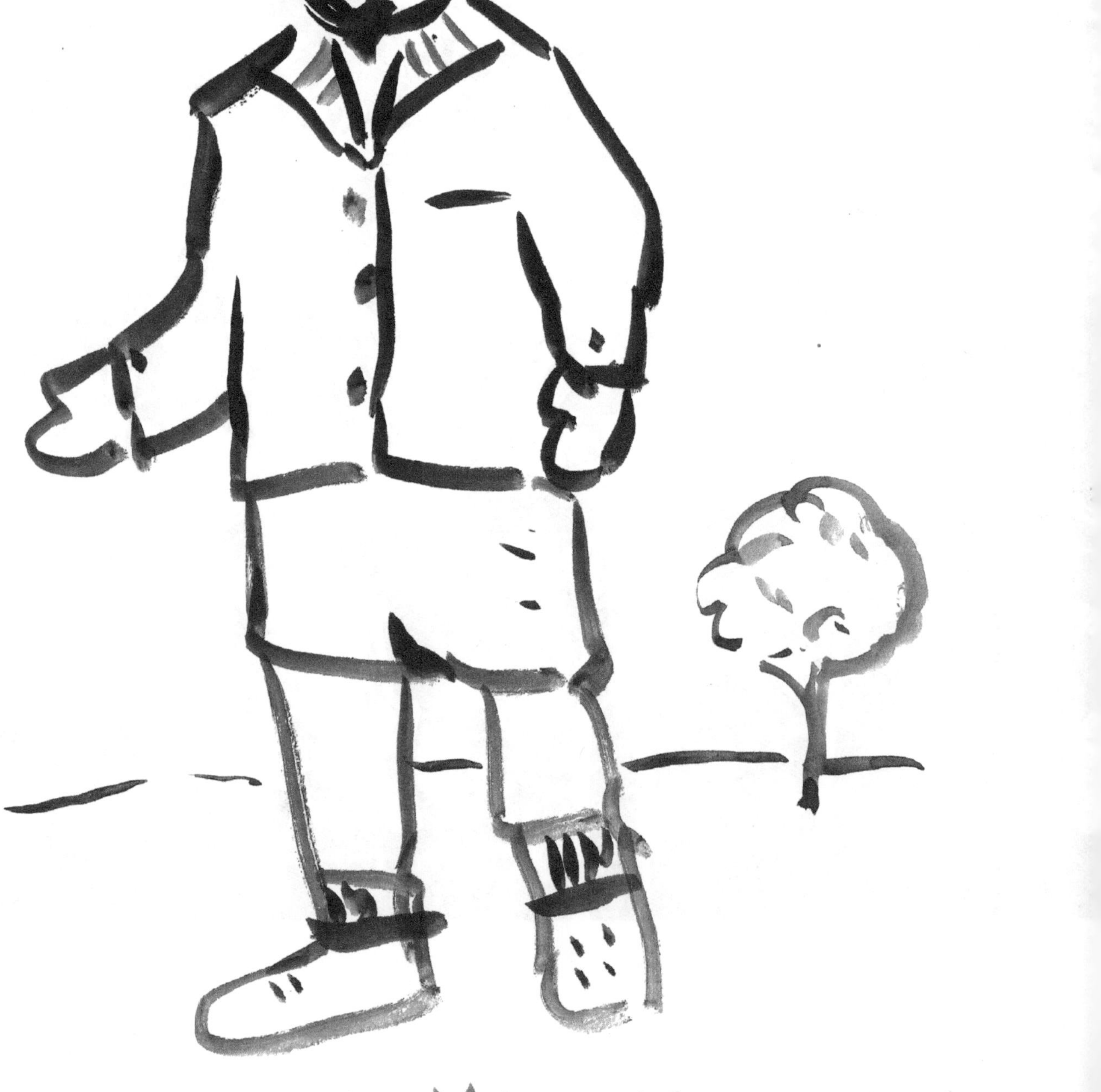

ME AS A YOUNG MAN

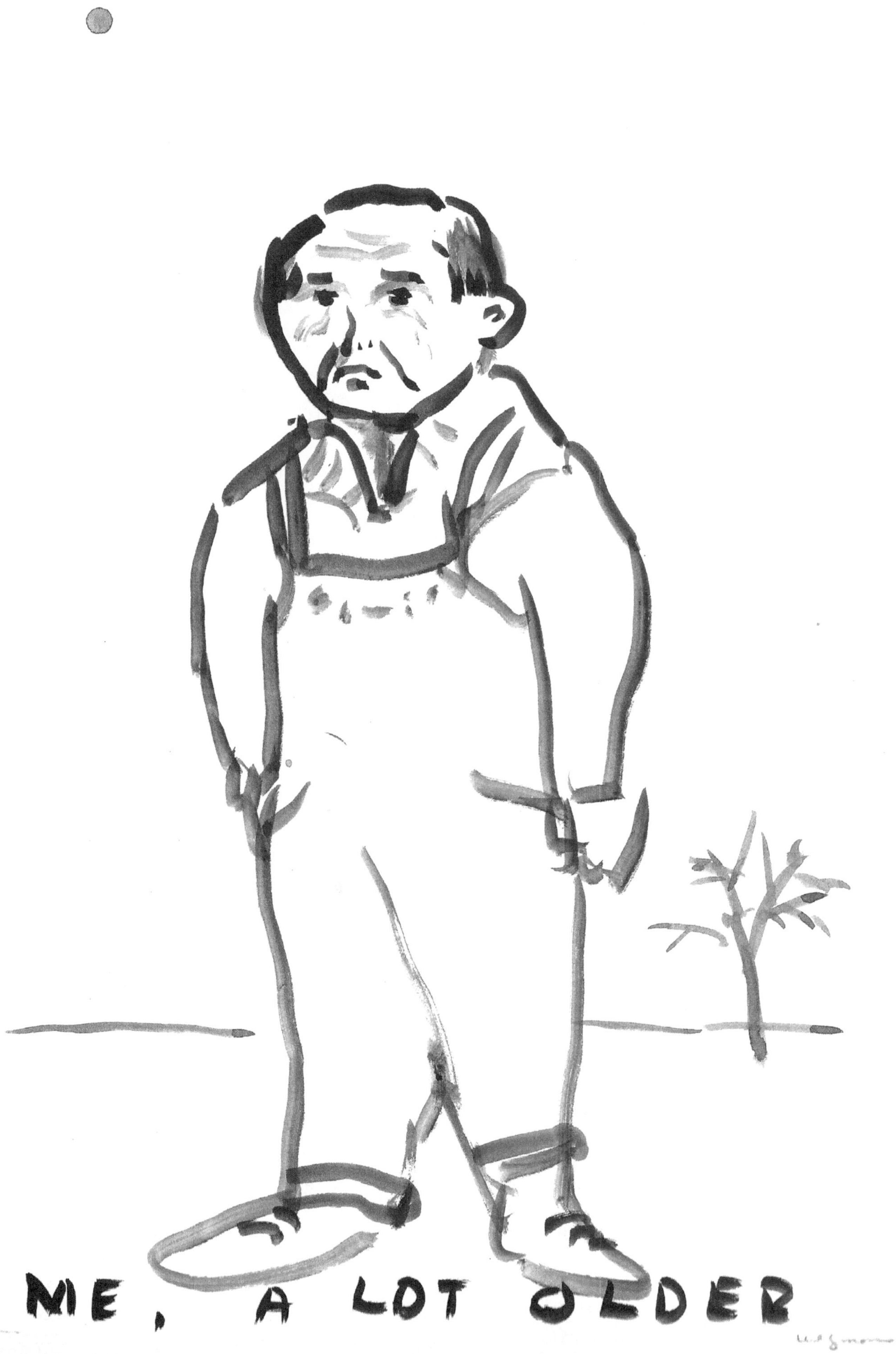
ME, A LOT OLDER

Martin Wilner

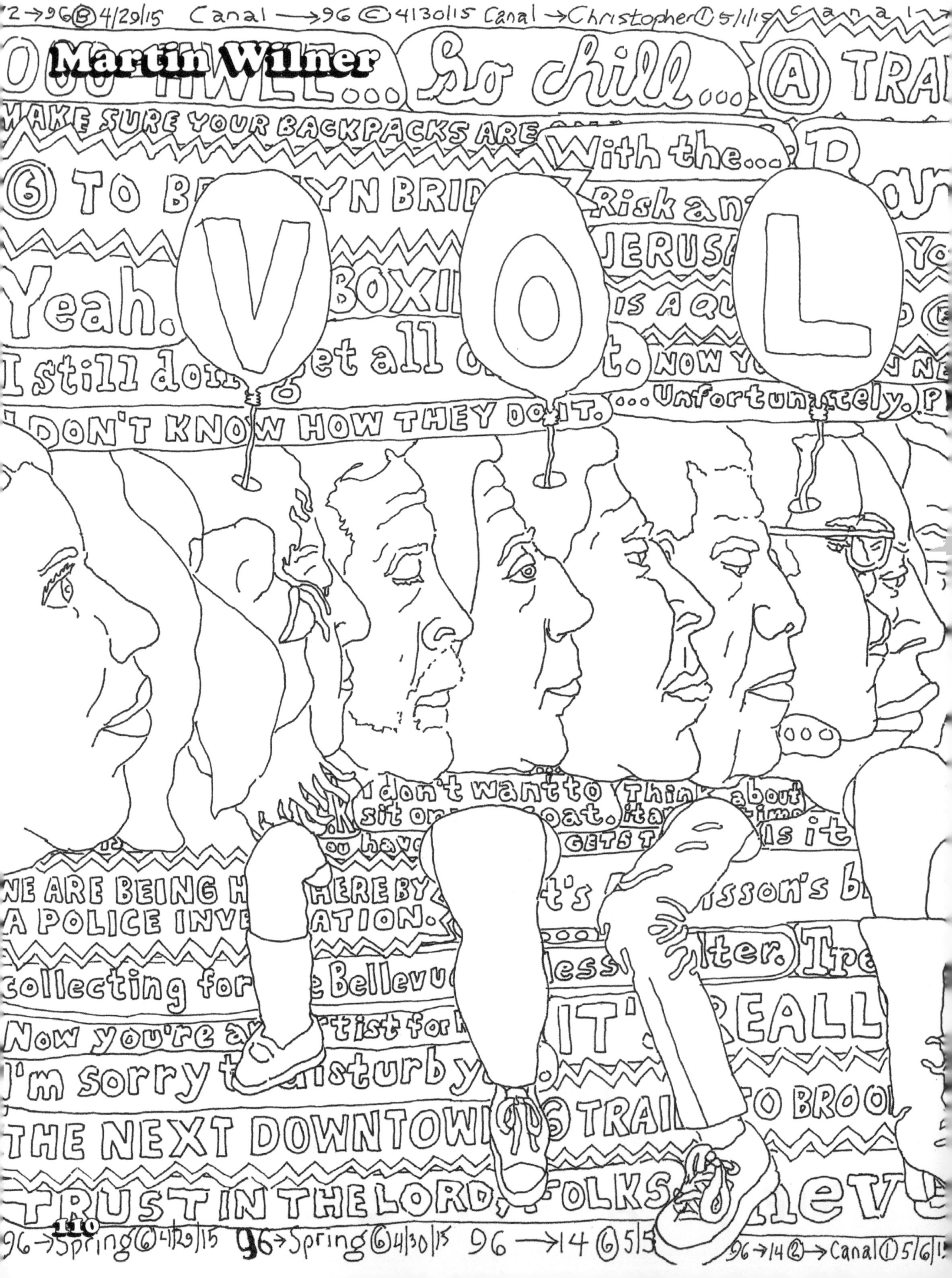

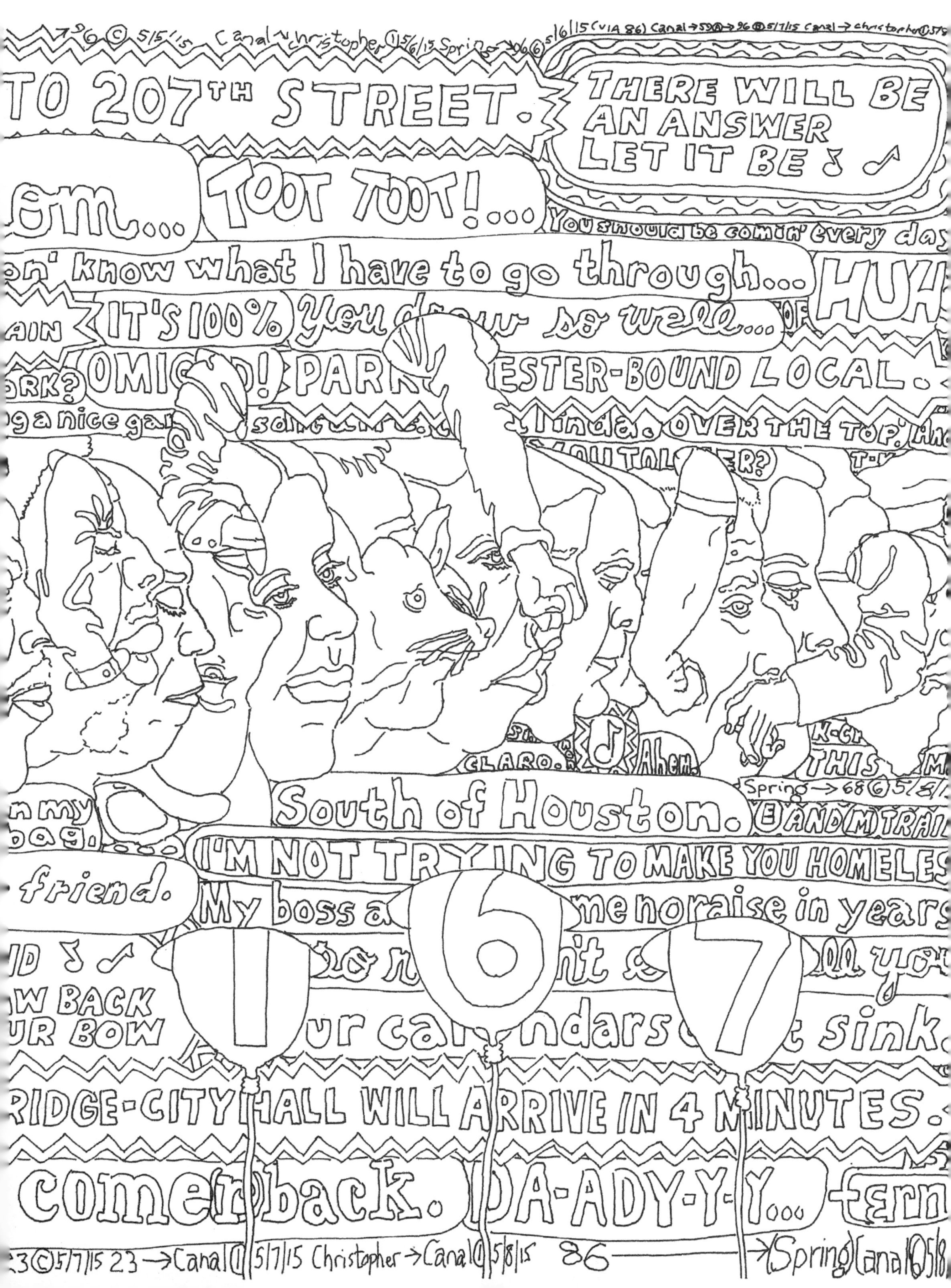
→96 © 5/5/15 Canal → Christopher ① 5/6/15 Spring → 96 ⑥ 5/6/15 (VIA 86) Canal → 59 Ⓐ → 96 ⑥ 5/7/15 Canal → Christopher ① 5/7
TO 207TH STREET.
THERE WILL BE AN ANSWER LET IT BE
om...
TOOT TOOT!...
You should be comin' every day
on' know what I have to go through...
HUH
AIN
IT'S 100%
You draw so well...
OMIG
PARK
ESTER-BOUND LOCAL.
ORK?
g a nice ga
linda.
OVER THE TOP.
CLARO.
Ahem.
THIS
Spring → 68 ⑥ 5/7/
n my bag.
South of Houston.
E AND M TRAI
I'M NOT TRYING TO MAKE YOU HOMELES
friend.
My boss a
me no raise in years
1
6
7
W BACK UR BOW
ur ca
ndars
sink.
RIDGE-CITY HALL WILL ARRIVE IN 4 MINUTES.
come back.
DA-ADY-Y-Y...
23 © 5/7/15 23 → Canal ① 5/7/15 Christopher → Canal ① 5/8/15 86 → (Spring) Canal ① 5/8

Jonas Wood

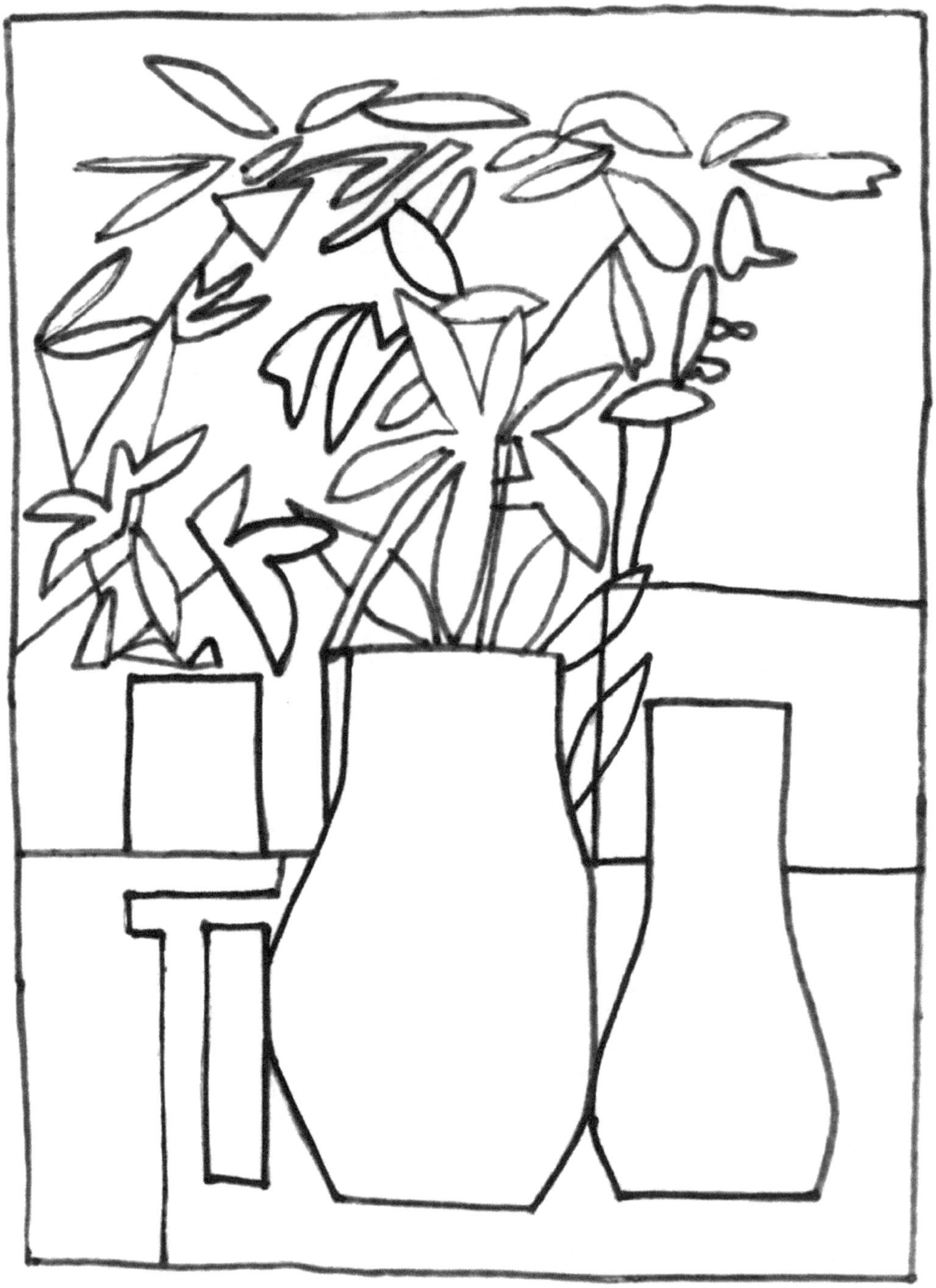

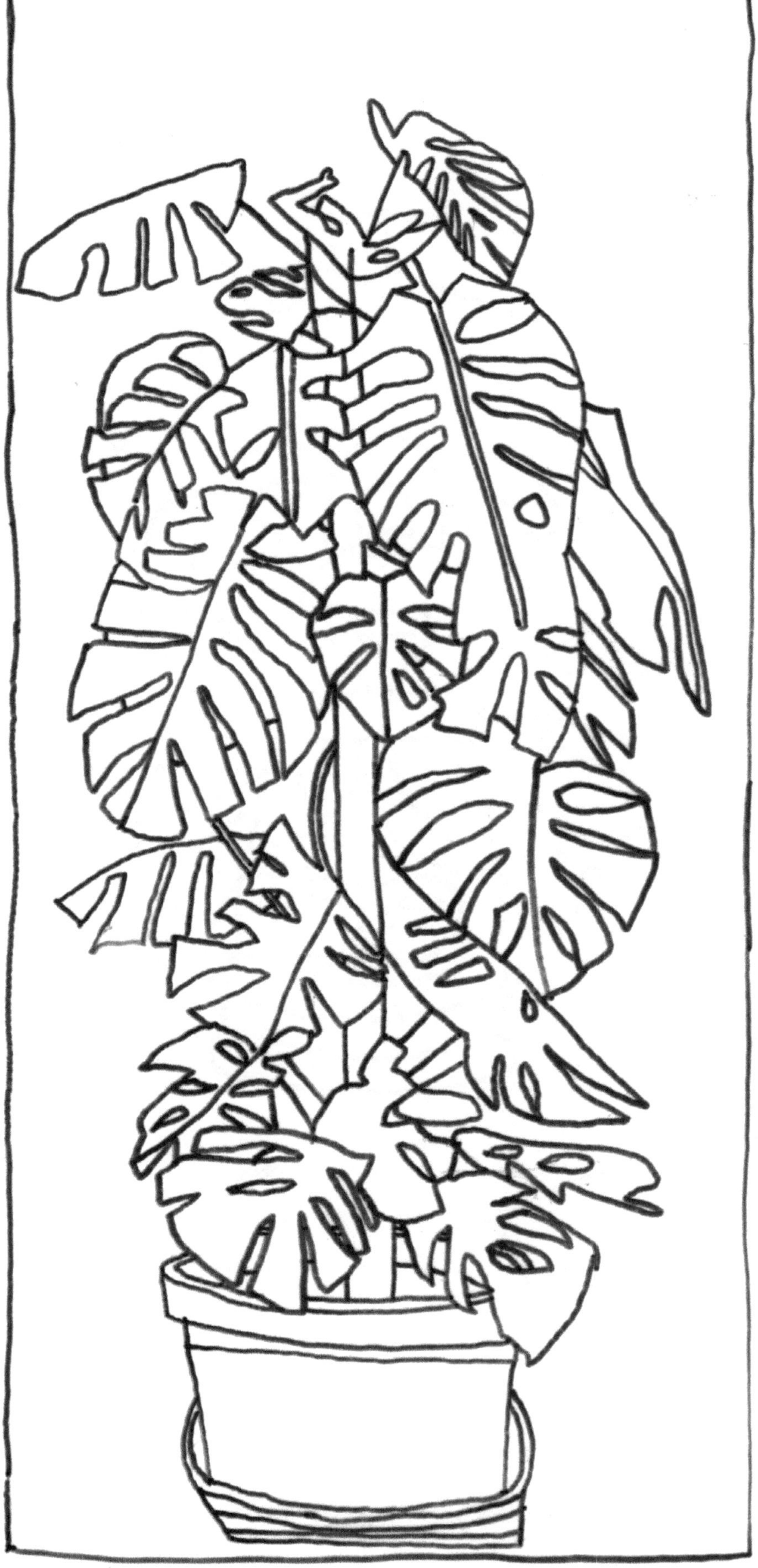

Saya Woolfalk

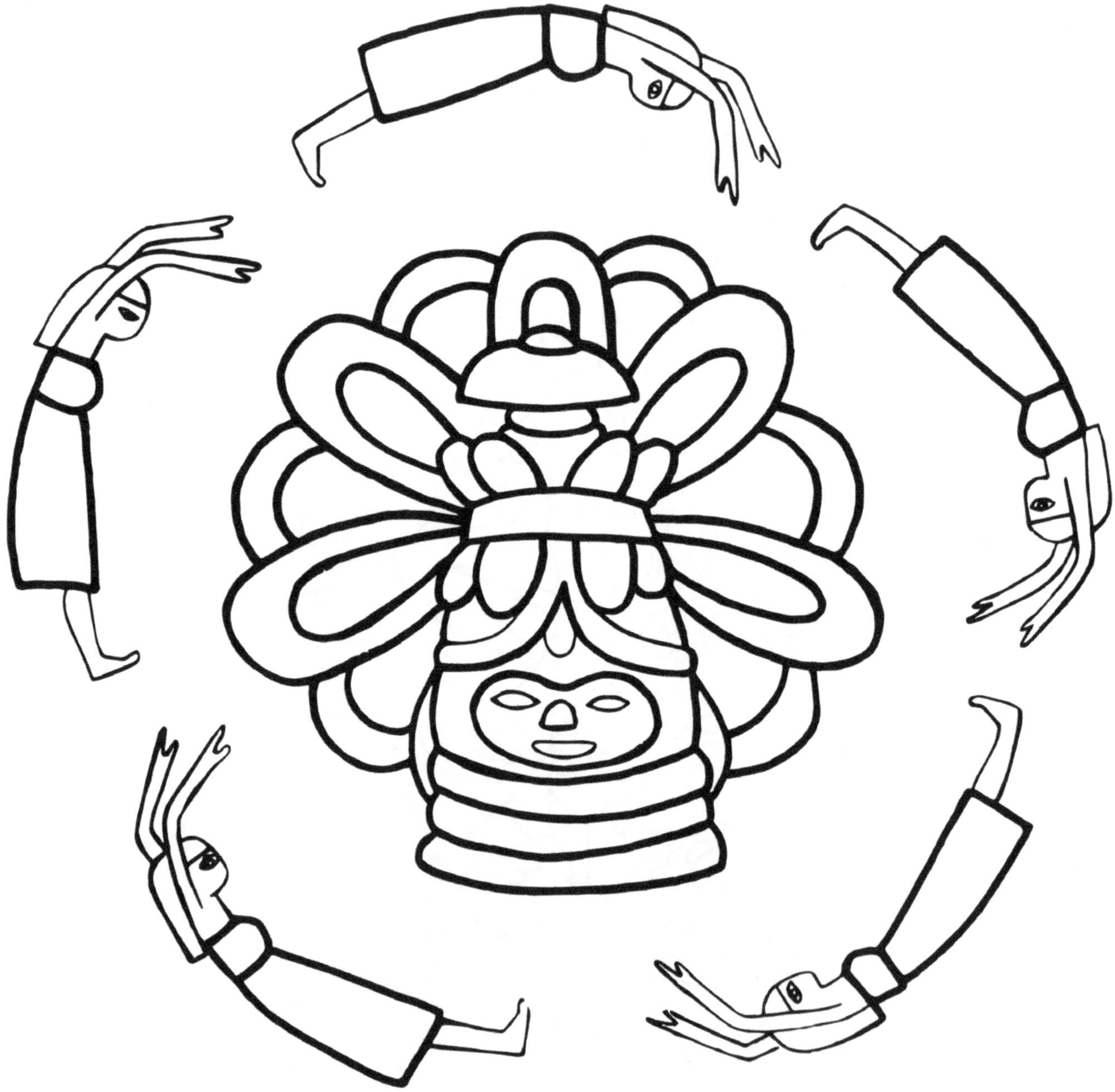

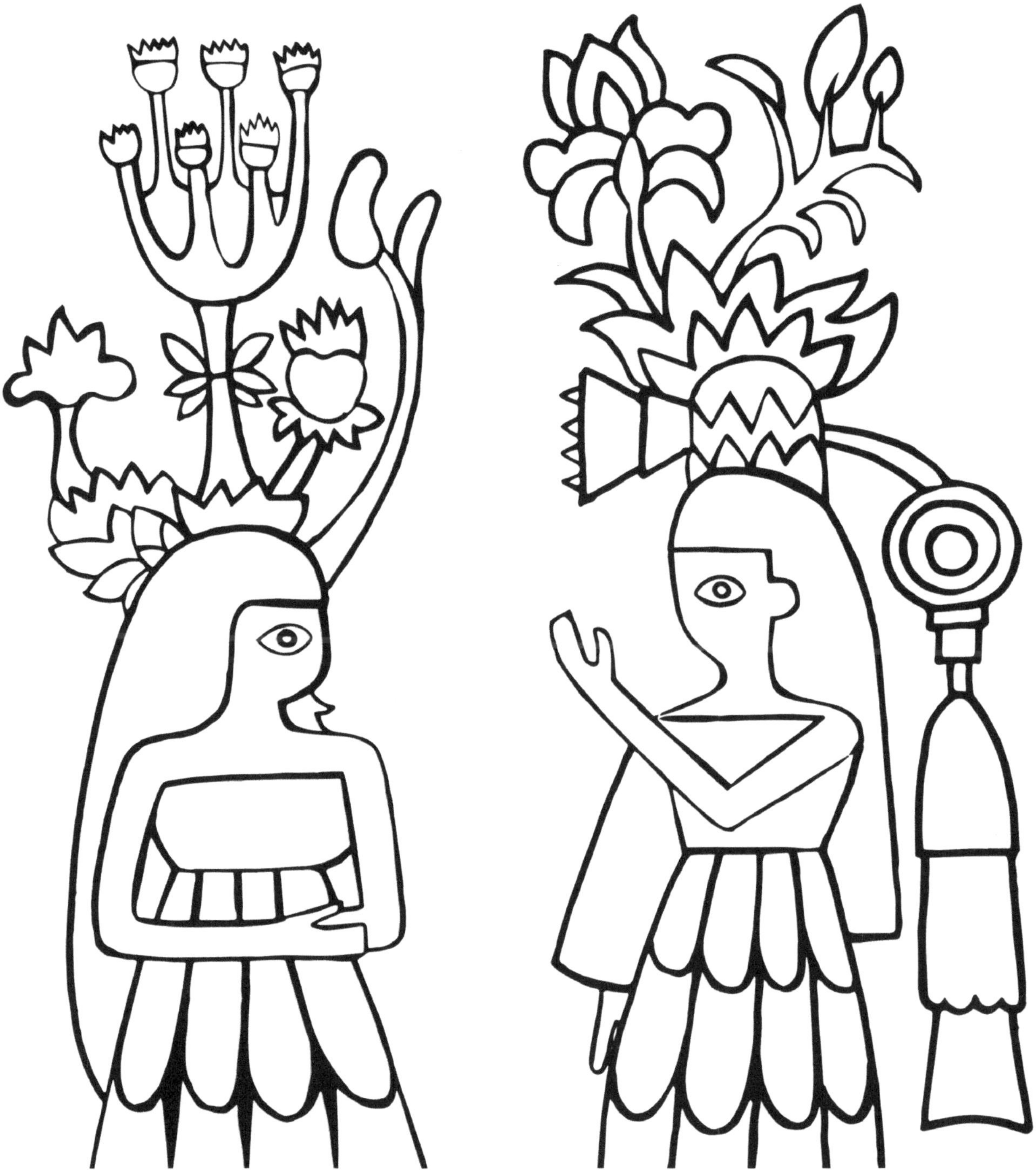

Your Art Here!

ARxT

Between the Lines: A Coloring Book by Contemporary Artists, Volume 5 **will be an inspiration to children of all ages and backgrounds, thanks to the boundless enthusiasm and originality the artists have brought to this project. It is through their generosity that this coloring book has been made possible.**

RxArt extends its most profound thanks to the artists, their studios, foundations and families. Additional thanks to the galleries and friends whose contributions and involvement have made this book a reality:

Rita Ackermann, Afruz Amighi, Andisheh Avini, John Baldessari, Barry X Ball, Ali Banisadr, Phyllida Barlow, Sanford Biggers, Olaf Breuning, Rebecca Chamberlain, Julia Chiang, Will Cotton, Ann Craven, Aaron Curry, N. Dash, Wim Delvoye, Claudia DeMonte, Kim Dingle, Mark Dion, Evan Gruzis, Subodh Gupta, Mark Hagen, Peter Halley, Keith Haring Foundation, Alex Israel, Rashid Johnson, Glenn Kaino, Wes Lang, Greg Lindquist, Liu Ye, Emil Lukas, Ed McGowin, Julie Mehretu, Malcolm Morley, Kambui Olujimi, Angel Otero, Tom Otterness, Erik Parker, Matthew Ritchie, Alexis Rockman, Ugo Rondinone, Kenny Scharf, Andrew Sendor, Alyson Shotz, Tom Slaughter, Josh Smith, Shinique Smith, Jennifer Steinkamp, William Wegman, Martin Wilner, Jonas Wood, Saya Woolfalk

Andrea Rosen Gallery, David Kordansky Gallery, Derek Eller Gallery, Gagosian Gallery, Gladstone Gallery, Gemini G.E.L., Hauser & Wirth, Honor Fraser, James Cohan Gallery, Lehmann Maupin, Leslie Tonkonow Artworks + Projects, Luhring Augustine, Marian Goodman Gallery, Sperone Westwater

RxArt would also like to convey its gratitude to the following individuals without whom this project would not have been realized: Eileen Jeng & Megan Skidmore of RxArt, Black Frame, Alexandra Gaty, Andrew Steinberg, Ali Winter, and Eric Wrenn.

This project was made possible with the generous support of Coach.

For more information about RxArt, please visit rxart.net.

Diane Brown
President

RxArt Inc.
208 Forsyth Street
New York, NY 10002
Tel 212 260 8797
Fax 212 260 8798
www.rxart.net

Rita Ackermann, *Red monkey without color*, © 2015 Rita Ackermann
Afruz Amighi, *Black Forest*, © 2015 Afruz Amighi
Andisheh Avini, *Untitled*, © 2015 Andisheh Avini
John Baldessari, *Noses & Ears, Etc.: The Gemini Series: Face with Nose and (Green) Ear*; © 2006 John Baldessari (Image adapted to coloring book format); *Noses & Ears, Etc.: The Gemini Series: One Face (Three Versions) with Nose, Ear, and Glasses*, © 2006 John Baldessari (Image adapted to coloring book format); *Sediment (Part Two): Duck and Chair*, © 2010 John Baldessari; *Sediment: Elton John's Smile and Portion of Shirt*, © 2010 John Baldessari
Barry X Ball, *Matthew Barney - Barry X Ball Decorated Dual Portrait*, © 2015 Barry X Ball
Ali Banisadr, *The Painter*, © 2015 Ali Banisadr
Phyllida Barlow, *untitled: balloons*, © 2015 Phyllida Barlow
Sanford Biggers, *Study No. 6*, © 2015 Sanford Biggers
Olaf Breuning, *Fish or Woman*, © 2010 Olaf Breuning; *I don't wanna know what is in my brain*, © 2010 Olaf Breuning
Rebecca Chamberlain, *Broken Windows, Diffused, Homatorium Series*, © 2015 Rebecca Chamberlain
Julia Chiang, *Everyone Says I Love You*, © 2015 Julia Chiang
Will Cotton, *Candy Forest*, © 2015 Will Cotton; *Macaron Hat*, © 2015 Will Cotton
Ann Craven, *Drawing (Clouds, 06-17-15), 2015*, © 2015 Ann Craven; *Drawing (Not Singing Yet, soon, with Cloud, 06-17-15), 2015*, © 2015 Ann Craven
Aaron Curry, *Untitled*, © 2015 Aaron Curry
N. Dash, *Untitled (For RxArt)*, © 2015 N. Dash
Wim Delvoye, *Dump Truck*, © 2014 Wim Delvoye
Claudia DeMonte, *The Luxury of Exercise*, © 2015 Claudia DeMonte
Kim Dingle, *Chicken Attack*, © 2015 Kim Dingle
Mark Dion, *The Young Ichthyologist*, © 2015 Mark Dion; *The Young Demonologist*, © 2015 Mark Dion
Evan Gruzis, *RxArt Pages*, © 2015 Evan Gruzis
Subodh Gupta, *Untitled*, © 2015 Subodh Gupta
Mark Hagen, *Drawing 1986–2015*, © 2015 Mark Hagen
Peter Halley, *Exploding Cell Comic Book*, © 2015 Peter Halley
Keith Haring, *Untitled*, 1986 © Keith Haring Foundation
Alex Israel, *Self Portrait Maze*, © 2015 Alex Israel
Rashid Johnson, *Run Palm*, © 2015 Rashid Johnson
Glenn Kaino, *Untitled*, © 2015 Glenn Kaino
Wes Lang, *Untitled*, © 2015 Wes Lang
Greg Lindquist, *Duke Energy's Dan River I and II*, © 2014 Greg Lindquist
Liu Ye, *Untitled*, © 2000 Liu Ye
Emil Lukas, *Bubbles*, © 2015 Emil Lukas
Ed McGowin, *FINISH THE SENTENCE*, © 2014 Ed McGowin
Julie Mehretu, *Image appropriated from: Migration Direction Map, 1996*, © 1996 Julie Mehretu
Malcolm Morley, *Soldier from Guardian, back view*, © 1994 Malcolm Morley; *HMS Soldier*, © 2012 Malcolm Morley
Kambui Olujimi, *Seesaw or Whale*, © 2007 Kambui Olujimi
Angel Otero, *Untitled (SK-KM)*, © 2013 Angel Otero; *High Applause*, © 2015 Angel Otero
Tom Otterness, *Three Little Pigs*, © 2015 Tom Otterness
Erik Parker, *RxArt Book Piece*, © 2015 Erik Parker
Matthew Ritchie, © 2015 Matthew Ritchie
Alexis Rockman, *Drainage: Day and Night*, © 2015 Alexis Rockman
Ugo Rondinone, *Untitled*, © 2015 Ugo Rondinone
Kenny Scharf, *WHOZNOZEIZIT*, © 2015 Kenny Scharf
Andrew Sendor, *The Resurrected Grandmaster Cryptologist*, © 2015 Andrew Sendor
Alyson Shotz, *filmstrip*, © 2015 Alyson Shotz
Tom Slaughter, *Papercut*, © 2014 Tom Slaughter
Josh Smith, *Mirror*, © 2015 Josh Smith
Shinique Smith, *Open Word Drawing*, © 2014 Shinique Smith
Jennifer Steinkamp, *Daisy Bell*, © 2015 Jennifer Steinkamp
William Wegman, *Young/Old*, © 2015 William Wegman
Martin Wilner, *Journal of Evidence Weekly Vol. 167*, © 2015 Martin Wilner
Jonas Wood, *Untitled*, © 2015 Jonas Wood
Saya Woolfalk, *Pollen Catchers*, © 2015 Saya Woolfalk

Design by Eric Wrenn Office, New York
Printed by Kappa Graphics

Between the Lines: A Coloring Book by Contemporary Artists, Volume 5